17x 3/10 -8/n
20x- 10/12 -6/17

House Beautiful

IT'S ALL IN THE DETAILS

House Beautiful

IT'S ALL IN THE DETAILS

A DECORATING WORKSHOP

TESSA EVELEGH

HEARST BOOKS
A Division of Sterling Publishing Co., Inc.
New York

Created, edited, and designed by
Duncan Baird Publishers Ltd.,
Castle House, 75–76 Wells Street, London W1T 3QH

Managing Editor: Emma Callery
Designer: Alison Shackleton

Library of Congress Cataloging-in-Publication Data

Evelegh, Tessa.
House beautiful, it's all in the details : a decorating
workshop / Tessa Evelegh. p. cm.
Includes index.
ISBN 1-58816-498-5
1. Decoration and ornament, Architectural, in interior
decoration. I. House beautiful. II. Title.
NK2115.5.A73E94 2006
729--dc22
2005026238

1 2 3 4 5 6 7 8 9 10

Published by Hearst Books
A Division of Sterling Publishing Co., Inc.
387 Park Avenue South, New York, NY 10016

www.housebeautiful.com

For information about custom editions, special sales,
premium and corporate purchases, please contact Sterling
Special Sales Department at 800-805-5489 or
specialsales@sterlingpub.com.

Distributed in Canada by Sterling Publishing
c/o Canadian Manda Group, 165 Dufferin Street
Toronto, Ontario, Canada M6K 3H6

Distributed in Australia by Capricorn Link
(Australia) Pty. Ltd.
P.O. Box 704, Windsor, NSW 2756 Australia

Manufactured in China

Sterling ISBN 13: 978-155816-498-8
ISBN 10: 1-58816-498-5

CONTENTS

FOREWORD

Reading through a pile of real estate particulars, it is always the details that bring a house alive for us: elegant fireplaces, beautiful ceilings, exquisite moldings. It's all the more obvious in period houses when the notes list the wealth of detail that has been retained or refurbished, bearing witness to a home that has been cared for and cherished over the years. Somehow, without the embellishments, a building simply does not stand out among the many in the ranks of its era. Add detail, and you add character. The right embellishments give a house integrity that everyone can recognize: one whose basic architecture and proportions are complemented by the details that count. But period homes don't have the monopoly on architectural embellishments. Modern architecture may be sleeker and more minimal than older styles, but it is still through the detail that a house moves from simply being a building to becoming a home with personality and style.

It's All in the Details is a book that is packed with information to help you add the correct finishing touches to your home, whatever its style and period. It aims to unravel the mysteries of embellishments and the period with which they are associated by looking at seven of the most important American styles and their development and then outlining the key details needed to create the look. The next chapter discusses different options for the details that run right through the house, including doors, windows, moldings, and floors.

Finally, in the "Room by Room" chapter, *It's All in the Details* looks at specific priorities plus any embellishments particular to that room. It's a

fascinating book for any homeowner, and an invaluable reference, whether you're building a new home, restoring an old one, or simply taking on a redecoration project.

Armed with this book, you can carry out initial research and take your time to assess what would be right for your home before even stepping over any suppliers' thresholds or discussing details with builders (who are generally more keen on fitting the easier option, rather than going the extra mile to find the correct one). You will be more than rewarded by your effort. For example, we recently witnessed an astounding improvement in a dark, uninspiring house of the 1920s. The owners added crown molding and replaced the windows and fireplaces. Oppressive low ceilings took on an elegant look once the original crown molding was matched and fitted; light poured more readily through the windows with fine muntins and frames closer in style to the originals than the clumsy replacements; and a sleek limestone fireplace mantel offered an elegant focal point, replacing the heavy, dark wood that was added in the Seventies. You don't have to go that far to make a difference, of course. You may simply want help with choosing light fixtures; guidance on the right kind of door; or you may want to immerse yourself in inspiration so you can be sure that the style is both comfortable and right for your home.

The Editors of *House Beautiful*

SCENE
SETTING

DETAILS, DETAILS

The original purpose of architectural detail was to cover up the join at the point where two materials met. So casings were devised to cover the point at which the doors and windows meet the wall; baseboards to cover the connection between the walls and floor; mantelpieces to beautify and seal the join between the wall and fireplace; and crown moldings to smooth the line between the walls and ceiling. Traditionally, these then became an ideal opportunity to add detail and embellishment, lending decorative depth to the room. The elegant simplicity of the eighteenth century took on an ever more elaborate feel: crown moldings became cornices with intricate friezes; pillars and pilasters were added to fireplaces and casings, and baseboards became deeper. By the end of the Victorian period, architectural embellishments were very elaborate. Moldings, stair parts, doors, and windows were mass-produced in a seemingly endless variety for homes across the country.

▶ **Doorway style**

Pretty glazed double doors bring architectural interest, adding individuality to an elegant Colonial house.

▼ **Arty balustrades**

The strong geometric shapes of these metal balusters have a distinct Fifties feel. Each one is different, arranged to make an interesting varied overall design.

SCENE SETTING

As a reaction to industrialization, the Arts and Crafts Movement developed in Europe, and the Beaux Arts movement spread to America from France, rekindling and nurturing the merits of craftsmanship. Houses often incorporated exquisite stained glass, wood carving, and metalwork. The inevitable reaction to this was to simplify, and aided by the unsustainable costs of hand-crafting, the Modern Movement was born. Modern architecture generally shuns embellishment but reveres fine materials and hardware. The aim is to design fine forms with clean lines for a clutter-free look that does not need extraneous decoration. With the Modern Movement, baseboards disappeared; cornices were replaced with shadow gaps between the walls and ceiling for a neat finish; closets became flush, masquerading as part of the walls; and knobs and handles shrunk to the sleekest and most discreet size possible, sometimes even disappearing altogether. However, these are all details that need decisions and are every bit as instrumental in the overall look of the room as the more flamboyant embellishments of earlier times.

▶ **Expressive ceiling**
Exposed rafters and beams add character to bedrooms under the roof eaves, expressing the structure of the building while bringing rugged texture to the room.

▶▶ **Eclectic detail**
The pillars and semi-curved walls in this room are pure Federal style, and although the plain ceiling is free of crown moldings and the built-in bookshelves are classic Modern, it works, given the link of Federal-style furniture.

STARTING OUT

The original features of a house are always those that make the design a harmonious whole, but these can be sacrificed to successive "refurbishments." Damaged moldings may have been removed rather than restored; wooden window frames replaced by plastic for ease of maintenance; and elements covered up with the introduction of central heating. Over the years, the cumulative effect of these losses erodes the look and integrity of the design until somebody with the vision and time can restore it to its former glory.

But where should you begin? First, you need to research what should be there. Quite apart from books like this one, specialty magazines, and libraries, there's a lot of firsthand research you can do. If you live in a city or fairly well-populated area, you can do this literally by walking up and down the road and noting any features

that are undoubtedly original. For example, where windows have been replaced, they do not always have the original configuration of panes or muntins. If you live in a more rural area, it is unlikely that you will find a house so closely similar to your own. However, you can note the details of houses that are of the same period.

When you can picture your house when it was new, you need to find replacements that are as close to the original as possible. Carpenters can make new windows to any dimensions, and supplied with the measurements of a neighbor's original, they could restore your house's façade. When it comes to crown moldings, baseboards, and other trimwork, all a carpenter or plaster worker needs is a sliver of the original, from which he can produce as much as you need. Even the most elaborate plaster work can be restored to its original glory.

◀ Dark looks

Dark-stained timber, such as these rafters and lintels, are typically Spanish style. They have been teamed with dark-stained Spanish-style furniture, though when it comes to the bed, comfort takes precedence over style with a supportive box spring and mattress.

▲ Clean simplicity

Simplicity rules when it comes to Modern style for a clean look and easy-living lifestyle: Flat profile window casings and baseboards not only look good, they are easy to keep clean, too. The angular lines of the fireplace have been reflected in the choice of dining table and chairs.

THE STYLE FILE

colonial

elegant

federal

swedish

sleek

spanish

modern

cozy

folk art

caribbean

feminine

MAKE YOUR CHOICE

American houses are defined not only by the period in which they were built, but also by the cultural influences of the original settlers. In some states, those are predominantly Swedish, German, Dutch, or English; in others further west and south, they may be Spanish or Mexican. The homes of the earliest frontier settlers were, by necessity, simple. There was no infrastructure, there were no architects, and there were few resources. Even the better houses were little more than cottages. But by the early 1700s, the Colonial style moved into a new Classical phase when local builders were able to obtain European pattern books which were used to build the grander houses. These same builders also built more modest dwellings, combining local styles with the new pan-European Classical look to create a tapestry of styles that together became the American vernacular.

By the start of the nineteenth century, America was training its own architects, who developed the Federal style from the current European Regency style. By the middle of the century, the plentiful supply of architects designed lavish mansions inspired by English Elizabethan manors, French châteaux, and Italian palazzi for wealthy clients who prospered in the post-Civil War era. Lasting into the early twentieth century, these styles were highly decorative and known collectively as the American Beaux Arts. These exclusive homes subsequently influenced the more modest new homes of the 1920s and 1930s. The following pages review six of the most important American styles spanning nearly 400 years. At the end of the chapter, the Modern style looks at embellishments for today.

▶ **Flooded with light**

Metal-framed windows were popular with twentieth-century Modern architects because they could be made with fine muntins for a sleek overall finish. These wall-to-wall windows introduce an outdoor feel to the room, flooding it with light.

COLONIAL (1607–1780)

The appeal of Colonial style is its unpretentious design that harks back to a simpler time before the Industrial Revolution ushered in the age of mass production. It was a time when natural local materials offered the only choices, and practicality took precedence over fashion. During the hard winters of the early Colonial years, there was no time for fussiness, and this expressed itself in buildings that had simple, elegant lines uncluttered by unnecessary embellishment.

Spanning almost two centuries, Colonial style is rooted in seventeenth-century English architecture. It ranges from the rustic appeal of the first settler homes to houses endowed with classical Georgian proportions. The look generally associated with Colonial is drawn from this period, when elegant mansions were built using designs published by English architects. The smooth lines of this early Georgian style have an elegance that transcends time, looking equally beautiful when furnished with the very best of modern design as with authentic Colonial originals.

The color palette

Authentic Colonial colors are all based on natural pigments in soft muted shades.

Green stone: Deep colors soak up the light and are best reserved for rooms mainly used in the evening.

Taupe: Slightly darker in shade than cream, the brown tones of this neutral color balance others that are more dominant.

Cream: A classic favorite, cream was a popular choice for the walls, and this color looks just as elegant now.

China blue: Easy to live with, this soft, muted blue was inspired by classic Chinese porcelain, introduced into Europe in the 1700s.

Muted yellow: A popular shade derived from earth pigments that had a sunny appeal. Its muted tone makes it a suitable color for all climates.

Blue gray: This soft, blue gray was popular in the early eighteenth century, adding a sophisticated tone.

▲ Easy dining

This light, relaxing dining room has many Colonial features: the paneled door, sash windows, and the molded cornice, which is brought out over the window to create a neat cornice box in keeping with the architecture.

Exposed beams are part of the original architecture of this Colonial house.

White-painted doors have graduated panels. The smaller panels at the top add the illusion of height.

Fireplace surrounds are typically decorative. This one is made up of panels that are painted white.

Simple molding adds decorative interest to an elegant fireplace surround.

Sash windows are typically divided into many small panes by narrow dividers called muntins.

The original pine floorboards have been given a dark stain and polish.

Painted paneled shutters are typical of the Colonial style.

▲ Colonial charm

Colonial style can elegantly combine the rustic simplicity of the early houses with Georgian features that were added at a later date. Here, a rudimentary beamed ceiling sits surprisingly well with elegant, cream paneled walls and fireplace. The key to success in this room is the dark oak floor, which teams well with the beams. Both have been left uncovered so that the rich patina of the wood can be fully enjoyed.

THE ESSENCE OF COLONIAL STYLE

The very earliest of Colonial houses were rudimentary wooden buildings, often paneled in unstained, unpainted pine with floorboards to match. Floors could be painted with handsome geometric designs or covered with painted floor cloths. Most settlers had movable furniture, and so built-in furniture was limited to simple shelving. As life became more settled and people more affluent, Colonial homes began to reflect the elegant Georgian styles that were currently popular in England. These later Colonial homes were much more refined, with painted paneling on walls which sometimes incorporated built-in closets. Toward the end of the era, the larger houses became more elaborate, with fireplaces that incorporated pilasters and ever more elaborate carving, reminiscent of Thomas Chippendale's European furniture.

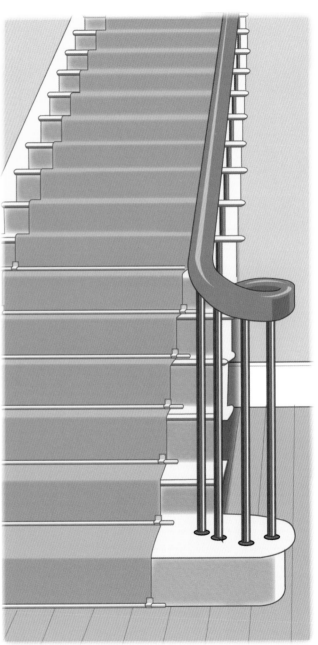

▲ Pure simplicity

This light, airy bedroom is typical of Colonial style with its elegant crown molding, wooden floor covered with a natural fiber carpet, and polished wood furniture.

Staircases

Typical Colonial staircases, such as this one, have turned balusters fixed to the stair ends which are often decoratively carved.

Windows

By the early eighteenth century, most windows were sash, featuring many small panes. This one has elaborate casings. Later styles in larger houses featured pilasters, arched windows, and window seats.

Fireplaces

Fireplaces were often set in paneled feature walls which could include elaborate chimneypieces, such as this one incorporating pilasters, a pediment, and cornice with egg-and-dart detailing.

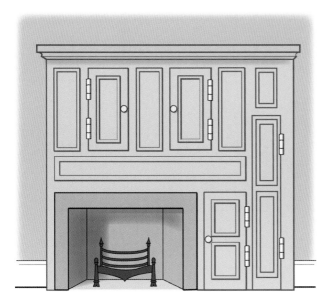

Built-in cupboards

Elaborate fireplace surrounds were typically paneled. Some panels could be cupboard doors, even above the fireplace. Fancier homes often had cupboards with glazed doors.

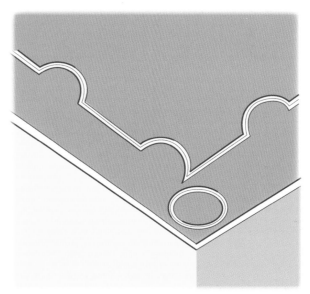

Ceilings

Early Colonial houses had exposed beams, but by the eighteenth century, ceilings were plastered and fitted with trimwork. Some in grander styles had additional moldings.

FOLK ART

A decorative rather than architectural style, Folk Art developed from the times of the early settlers. Houses in country districts were simple and constructed from available local materials. To disguise rough plaster, walls were often fully or half paneled with a chair rail on top. In an effort to make their houses more refined, people decorated the walls and floors, usually by hand, because there were few machines or factories. However, there were plenty of available resources. Panels could be decorated using a theorem painting made up of several different stencils to create an elaborate still life that perfectly fitted the space. Traveling craftsmen would sell punched tinware wall sconces and containers. Metal fittings, such as chandeliers, weathervanes, and painted oil cloths to soften wood floors.

The color palette

The restful shades of natural pigments make up the Folk Art palette. Most are derived from local earth tones, giving these homes a natural sense of belonging in their surroundings. This also meant that the palette could differ slightly, depending on the locality.

Yellow: This muted earth yellow is a traditional color that works well with Folk Art style.

Blue: This greeny blue regularly appears in original Folk Art style, and its introduction adds authenticity to modern equivalents.

Earth: The terra-cotta and red hues in earth pigments introduce a range of natural, bright but warm tones to the palette.

Olive: Another earth tone, this green hue is perfect for painted paneling, making a restful backdrop.

Light blue: Although we think of Folk Art colors as muted, a lighter blue like this was often introduced in small quantities to introduce a livelier feel.

Cream: The soft tones of cream and off-white always team well with the muted Folk Art palette. Use them for painting woodwork or for walls where a lighter look is desired.

▲ **Folk Art charm**
Highly individual, yet undeniably Folk Art in style, this light and airy landing is filled with interest. The fretwork balustrades bring a pretty motif to the whole stairway, while the walls display variety in both color and texture.

This exquisite hand-painted mural depicts old New York in typical Folk Art style, covering all the upper part of the wall.

The leaf detail around the hanging lamps displays the charming simplicity and effectiveness of Folk Art decoration.

Metal weathervanes were Folk Art staples, but they were usually kept outside.

Molded half panels protect the lower part of the wall. Here, they have been painted in the palest cream to lighten the room.

▲ **One of a kind**

This hand-painted mural brings a unique quality to this Folk Art room. The overall effect is both cozy and intimate.

THE ESSENCE OF FOLK ART

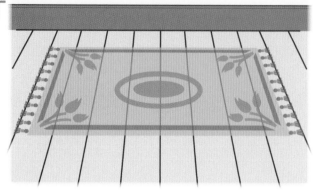

It's the decorative detail that identifies authentic Folk Art style more than the particular architecture, though the emphasis is more relaxed country style than city smart. The key is plenty of hand-painted, handcrafted detail. Walls could be paneled or plastered; they're also very likely to be decorated with a stenciled or stamped border or with a hand-painted mural. Bare floorboards are softened with an oil cloth or hand-hooked rag rug. Plain wooden doors may have the decorative detail of a heart cutout or other motif. In turn, closet doors may be given punched tinware panels, or the wooden panels may be decorated with calligraphy, simple flowers, fruits, or animals.

Floor cloths

Hand-painted floor cloths added decoration. Craftsmen often made these to order, and their work frequently portrayed favorite Pennsylvania Dutch motifs, such as tulips.

▲ Today's folk

The quilts used as hangings and simple, homey motifs on the upholstery all bear witness to pure Folk Art style, as does the dollhouse and hand-painted container.

Punched tinware

Flowers, fruits, and birds were popular motifs, and these often appeared on punched tinware, used as cupboard panels, wall sconces, and lanterns.

Stenciling

Stencils and stamps are an easy way to apply decoration to walls. Sometimes, they were simply used to create a framework to an alcove, door, or window, as here, or they were used to cover the entire wall.

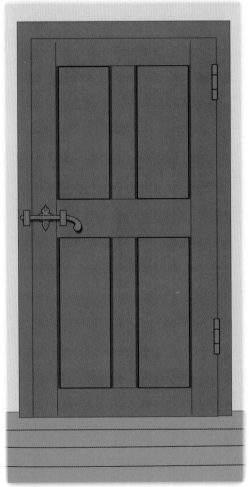

Theorem paintings

This was another form of decoration, often applied to door panels, as on this large kitchen cupboard. Artisans composed theorem paintings from a series of separate stencils that could be combined in any number of ways to create a unique still life. In this case, the bowl, the fruits, leaves, bird, and butterfly represent individual motifs that the artist could arrange as he or she liked.

Doors

Simple paneled doors—either in natural wood or painted—are framed with unembellished casings and have wrought-iron hardware.

FEDERAL AND EMPIRE (1780–1850)

Elegant and refined, Federal homes transcend fashion and are universally desirable. The era was influenced by the British Regency and French Empire styles that harked back to Roman and Greek classicism, featuring fine curved and elliptical architectural features and embellishments. Influenced by the Scottish brothers, Robert and James Adam, decorative molding during the Federal period became ever more elaborate, featuring garlands, foliage, festoons, egg and dart, and Greek key designs along with cornucopia, urns, and fruit baskets. In America, the eagle symbol of the new Federal government became a popular motif.

Until this time, all building design had been undertaken by carpenters, adapting published European pattern books. But in the early nineteenth century, the new profession of classically trained architect began to develop in America. The result was a maturing American Federal style that was simpler yet more elegant than its European cousin, the Regency style.

The color palette

Clear bright hues express the design confidence that emerged during the Federal era.

Vibrant green: Typically Federal, this green became a fashionable color for dining rooms. Light reflective, yet far from pastel, it exudes a sureness of style.

Blossom: Used more for trimmings and detail, this muted mid-tone pink adds softness to an otherwise strident palette.

Gold: A wonderfully uplifting color for walls and exquisite fabrics such as silk, gold is like a yellow with extra winning strength.

Spice: A lively earth tone, this spicy shade looks good in larger rooms with plenty of natural light.

Blue: A sophisticated shade of mid-tone blue with subtle green undertones, this is a surprisingly easy color to live with.

Cream: Used mainly for woodwork, cream can also provide a fine backdrop for Federal architecture.

▲ Curved elegance

Curved walls with recessed panels and other molded details demonstrate the sophisticated nature of Federal architecture.

This generous cornice has simple low-profile molding, typical of the period.

The Federal style adopted the paned sash window as its standard and popularized the stucco detailing on the window head.

A mainstay of Federal style is the **Greek key design** often seen as a detail on cornices and moldings.

The **neo-Roman bust** is a typical Federal emblem.

Deep baseboards with fine, restrained molding suit the generous proportions of Federal houses.

▲ Federal elegance

With overtones of Classical Roman architecture, fine proportions, and elegant detailing, Federal style is universally aspirational.

THE ESSENCE OF FEDERAL STYLE

Federal style, like its English counterpart, Regency, took classic Georgian architecture and refined it. Corinthian and Ionic columns stood sentry wherever possible—around doors, windows, and arches. Doors, windows, and even some fireplaces had pediments, offering a sense of grandeur. Simple Georgian moldings were replaced with much more elaborate details, ranging from pastoral urns to Classical motifs, such as Greek key designs, acanthus leaves, victorious chariots, and the Federal eagle. The designs became elongated and of lower relief for a more elegant look than those of the Georgian style. Crown moldings, casings, and mantelpieces were adorned, sometimes with simple reed-and-tie molding teamed with corner roundels; or with elaborate rows of molding that could incorporate six or more motifs. The wooden floors were decoratively painted or enhanced with inlaid borders. Reception rooms featured ornate paneling while grander homes had elaborate pilasters, corbels, and plaster moldings around arches, between rooms, or in the hallway.

Windows
The classic Federal windows were sash windows with six panes over six panes and thinner muntins than their Colonial predecessors. The most elaborate incorporated classical pilasters, pediments, and arched tops, as here.

Staircases
Graceful spirals and ellipses were a hallmark of Federal style. Close-set, square-profile balusters like these, sweeping around the curves, served to accentuate the elegance of the architecture.

Crown moldings

In grander houses, crown moldings could consist of many elements with different motifs, as here.

Fireplaces

The swan-neck pediment at the top of this fireplace was also seen over doors or windows. Elaborate overmantels like this were the mark of a grand home, while pilasters and eagle motifs were seen even in modest homes.

Doors

The Federal period was one time when door and window casings weren't necessarily mitered. Simple trims with roundel blocks at the corners were a typical form, framing paneled doors.

THE STYLE FILE

SWEDISH STYLE

Swedish style mirrors eighteenth-century European style. It dates to the reign of Gustav III, who returned to Sweden in 1771 to take the throne after two years in Versailles, where he had developed a passion for the then-current Neo-classicism. He influenced the Swedish interpretation of the elaborate Louis XVI styles, simplifying them and adding elements from England, Germany, and Holland.

What we now know as Swedish style can range from the elegance of courtly Gustavian homes to the simplicity of country dwellings. It was a look that was revived at the beginning of the twentieth century by the Swedish painter Carl Larsson, who illustrated the home that he and his wife, Karin, made together in the village of Sundborn. The elegant, light-filled look has seen another revival in recent years with its huge influence on the popularity of shabby chic, a style which depends largely on the furniture shapes and architectural detailing of Swedish style.

The color palette

Soft tones of light-reflective colors teamed with flashes of stronger red make Swedish style easy to live with as it sits in harmony with today's lifestyles.

Ash gray: This softest of grays was commonly used to paint furniture. It is still an ideal shade both for walls and furniture in today's homes.

Fern: Soft green gray looks elegant in living rooms, or used in smaller quantities on furniture.

Georgian blue: This greeny blue shade was a favorite all over Europe in the eighteenth century. It has an intensity of color while retaining a light-reflective quality.

Red: Red and white checks were often used for furnishing fabrics and bed linens, adding a bright splash.

Taupe: This soft grayish beige is surprisingly light reflective. It provides the perfect background for many different color schemes.

Cream: The key to Swedish style, cream is used on walls, furniture, and even floors.

▲ Feminine touch

The simple fireplace surround is very much in the Swedish style: generous proportions teamed with restrained molding. The pretty bow detail on the mirror combined with low-profile reeding are classic Swedish style.

Windows have multiple small panes with fine muntins. Sash windows with six-over-six lights are the most common.

Pale floorboards add to the light and airy feel. These have been painted in a diamond pattern using off-white and palest gray.

Turned chair legs echo the Swedish style used for balusters.

▲ Swedish light

This is European eighteenth-century style at its simple best. The moldings are less fussy than in other styles for an overall elegant look. With walls, floors, and furniture all painted in the palest of shades, the effect is light, airy, and easy to live with.

THE ESSENCE OF SWEDISH STYLE

Developed in Scandinavia where winters are harsh, nights long, and daytime limited, light is a priority of Swedish style. Furniture, walls, and even floors, painted in off-whites and palest grays, reflect the light for bright, easy-to-live-in rooms. Set against architecture that's most easily described as refined Colonial, the key to the Swedish look is simplicity with feminine touches. Moldings are restrained, though they show a little embellishment in the form of simple garlands or a single bow. It's a look that has an unmistakable signature running through homes, no matter how sophisticated or simple. This is the appeal that makes Swedish style so translatable into today's interiors.

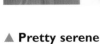 **Pretty serene**

The combination of cool light colors, simple moldings and curvy, feminine shapes has ensured the popularity of Swedish style over more than two centuries.

Doors

Paneled doors are the Swedish norm. They were often part glazed, as here, to allow light to shine into darker parts of the house.

Windows

City or country, windows were composed of numerous small panes with fine muntins. City windows were usually sash with folding shutters; country styles were more likely to be casement with simple shutters of tongue and groove boards, like these.

Walls

City Swedish houses had paneled walls that were painted. In simpler country homes, this was interpreted as beaded board with a plate shelf.

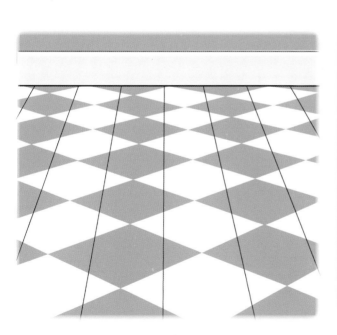

Floors

The favored material underfoot was wooden floorboards, generally painted in pale colors to reflect as much light as possible and bring decorative interest to the room.

Storage

Floor-to-ceiling cupboards with paneled doors made good use of space. In smaller homes, every corner was put to good use, even a shallow space over the fireplace, as here.

CARIBBEAN STYLE

More of a lifestyle than an architectural style, the Caribbean look is born of an unlikely marriage between the European fashion of the sugar plantation owners and the colorful expression of their African slaves. In the early days, both groups regarded their Caribbean home as temporary, but as sugar brought greater and greater wealth to the owners, their homes took on a more permanent air. They turned to their original European homelands for the inspiration of grander dwellings, while the slave population poured all they could in terms of color and decoration into their cabins—their only refuge from a brutal life.

Ranging from modest tin-roofed dwellings to Palladian grandeur, these opposite styles are united in their celebrations of the joys of the vibrant natural colors, embracing deep blue seas, lush green mountains, and brilliant golden sunshine. Combined with high ceilings and galleried verandas, the end result is vivacious and relaxing.

The color palette

An extrovert combination of vibrant hues is the hallmark of Caribbean homes. Although these colors are usually employed on the outside of houses, they do sometimes creep inside.

Olive green: This surprisingly muted shade makes an ideal foil for the rest of the lively Caribbean palette.

Provence blue: Introduced by French settlers, this is a favorite shade throughout the Caribbean.

Pink: This soft fresco shade offsets the whole delightful Caribbean palette of paintbox colors.

Turquoise: Turquoise celebrates the Caribbean light, working well with blues, pinks, and purples.

Soft red: At its best, this red looks like sun-bleached crimson. Details on walls and floors can be picked out in the brightest of reds.

Golden yellow: Not the soft, buttery shade so loved by northern Europeans, this dazzling gold is often teamed with red, turquoise, or olive green.

New dimensions
This twentieth-century house fuses modern minimalism with bright Caribbean tropical colors and a refreshingly cool stone floor.

Restrained crown molding, redolent of all elegant nineteenth-century houses, adds a sense of grandeur to the room.

White walls are typical Caribbean: colors are more commonly used for the outsides of the houses.

Painted louvered doors are the essence of Caribbean style. They are a popular design as they encourage air flow while shading the room from bright midday sun. The bottom portion of the door is paneled to provide strength to the door in the area where it is most likely to be knocked.

▲ Plantation echoes

This modern Caribbean dining pavilion incorporates many details typical of an elegant nineteenth-century Caribbean house. Situated beside a swimming pool, the overall effect is cool, light, and airy.

The stone floor makes for cool living. Its sturdiness is such that it could even outlast the house.

Fluted pillars bring a Classical feel to the room. The louvered doors, latticework, and pillars combine to create a screen effect.

Painted wood latticework is a decorative feature that is seen on balconies, verandas, and porches throughout the islands.

THE ESSENCE OF CARIBBEAN STYLE

Modest or grand, there are several elements that run through the Caribbean style, designed to shield the sun and facilitate the circulation of cool air. Prosaic as these aims might seem, the influence of African flamboyance has interpreted them in a highly decorative way, while the European plantation owners expressed them within their own classic styles. Louvered doors and windows, elaborate fretwork, decorative balustrades, and cool stone or wooden floors, along with a vibrant palette of colors (see page 36), are the hallmarks of Caribbean style. It's a style that has grown without self-consciousness and matured with the particular lifestyle of the islands. Modern Caribbean homes have simplified some of the more decorative elements, but they still lack pretension and, most important, they have retained the joyous color palette.

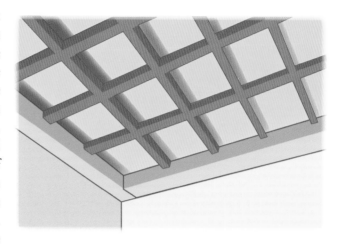

Ceilings

Caribbean ceilings are often high to encourage greater cooling airflow. Simple geometric moldings or exposed beams transform these into an important feature.

▲ Cool simplicity

Sleeker than traditional Caribbean houses, this Modern house incorporates the vibrant palette of coral, yellow, and aqua, so typical of island style.

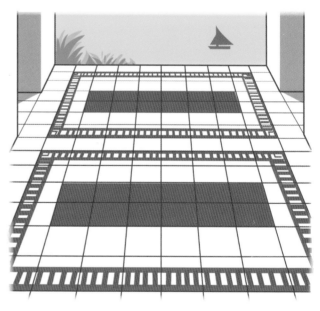

Floors

Floors are generally made of wood or tiles, which can range in material and style from plain stone to geometric patterns of glazed ceramic.

Doors

Many doors have louvered panels. This one has a solid lower panel to provide strength where it's needed. The louvers on the top two panels allow for greater air circulation while shielding the bright midday sun.

Fretwork

Ornate fretwork is a feature of Caribbean houses; it provides filtered light as well as decorative detail.

Windows

Louvered shutters adorn most Caribbean windows, which range from the simplest of openings to the grandest Palladian styles. Semicircular window tops are typical.

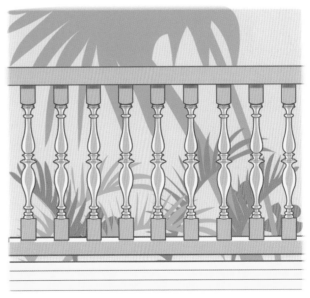

Balustrades

Balustrades are an essential element of Caribbean houses. Balusters are often traditionally turned, like these, though simple square and ornately fretworked are also popular.

SPANISH STYLE

Spanish architecture in America dates to the arrival of the Spanish conquistadors in the sixteenth century, and so can be considered one of the major vernacular styles. It went on to become established in the Spanish settlements in the Southwest, where the architecture suited the hot, dry climate.

The original Spanish style with its hallmark archways, white-painted interiors, and elaborate ceramic tiles is Moorish in influence, reflecting the 400 years during which Spain was ruled by the Islamic Moors. The look enjoyed a huge boost in popularity during the West Coast Spanish revival of the 1920s and 1930s and remains a popular style today. The classic Spanish look incorporates elaborately carved embellishments of dark wood, such as doors, window frames, and balustrades, while modern tastes prefer a lighter look, such as wrought-iron screens, white-painted archways, and terra-cotta floor tiles.

The color palette

White walls, terra-cotta floors, dark architectural wood: for a little flamboyance, introduce highly decorated ceramic tiles.

Terra-cotta: Floors are often tiled in terra-cotta, echoing the roof tiles outside.

Dark wood: Used for doors, window frames, shutters, beams, corbels, and pilasters, dark wood makes a huge impact on Spanish interiors.

White: Interior walls are almost always white, a cool reflective foil for the intense sun.

Blue/gold: Deep blue was much favored by the Moors. Here, it's offset by gold, a classic Spanish combination.

Blue/lemon: Lighter, brighter hues combined with the fresh design is an example of modern Spanish style.

Turquoise blue/yellow: A lively and favorite Spanish combination that brings color to simple interiors.

Blue/gold/terra-cotta/olive: Two blues and gold teamed with muted terra-cotta and green make a classic combination.

▲ Carving a niche

Carved dark wood is a hallmark of Spanish style. This elaborately carved bed makes a striking feature, and provides all the decoration needed in a plain white room. Reminiscent of Moorish design, carving is used throughout the interior: on beams, doors, windows, and columns.

Exposed beams express typical Spanish style and bring interesting dimension to the ceiling.

Carved wood adds detail interest and beauty to pillars, beams, doors, and windows.

A favorite decorative feature of Spanish style, builders used **wrought iron** for screens, gates, doors, and at windows.

Both in Adobe and traditional styles, **white walls** are the universal Spanish choice.

Terra-cotta is invariably used for roofing tiles, and this is often echoed inside with the use of terra-cotta floor, wall, or surface tiles. Here, it is introduced by a row of giant planters.

Cool **stone** is the preferred Spanish floor.

◀ **Adobe masterpiece**
The style of this Adobe Spanish home is lighter and more relaxed than the traditional northern style. The elements are similar, but for an easy-living, outdoor look the wood is left natural rather than finished with a dark stain.

THE ESSENCE OF SPANISH STYLE

White-painted walls, curved archways—both inside and out—pretty wrought-iron screens, and hand-painted ceramic tiles are the universal vocabulary of Spanish style. However, within that framework the look can vary quite dramatically. The Adobe style, with its fluid, white-painted forms, bleached timber, and ceramic tile floors, is especially popular in New Mexico, while the more classic dark wood floors and squarer architectural details, such as fireplaces, are typical of the Spanish Colonial revival of the 1920s. More recently, Spanish-style homes have taken on a much lighter feel, relinquishing the dark wood but retaining light, airy, white-painted rooms with elegant archways and cool, terra-cotta floors.

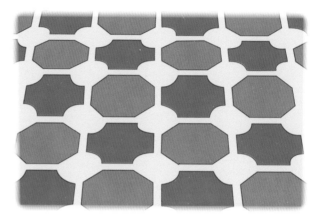

Floors
Terra-cotta tiles are a popular choice for floors. Here, terra-cotta octagons are interspersed with glazed blue tiles for added interest.

▲ Adobe fireside
Smooth fireplaces of white plaster are typical Adobe style. This one is complemented by the carved wooden beam, a universal Spanish architectural element.

Stairways
Brightly colored painted tiles are often used to enliven the interior. Adorning the risers of stone stairways is highly effective as it introduces color to floors.

Wrought iron

Screens and detailing in decorative scrolled designs of wrought iron comprise some of the principal delights of Spanish style.

Fireplaces

These can range from Adobe styles, as seen on the previous page, to the more formal Spanish Colonial revival styles of the 1920s. This one has hand-painted tiles.

Doors

Wooden doors with raised moldings find use both inside and out. The door hardware is often heavy wrought iron to complement the ornate wood carving.

Windows

Arched windows with dark wood frames set into deep reveals express essential design elements of Spanish style. Carved wooden shutters echo other internal wood details.

MODERN STYLE

The Modern Movement was born in the 1920s as architects reacted to what they perceived as the over-adornment of the Victorian age. Baseboards, wainscoting, picture rails, moldings, and elaborately carved wood disappeared. Stairways swept through houses in serpentine fashion, evoking the clean lines of passenger liners. In America, Frank Lloyd Wright stood out as the most influential Modern Movement architect, rejecting traditional design which was dominated by the European styles of centuries past.

Modern Movement architects on both sides of the Atlantic eschewed over-embellishment. It was an exciting era, but one that many did not understand, and on the domestic front, few embraced. Perhaps as a reaction against the swift march of change during the second half of the twentieth century, there was a yearning for a return to Classicism and a demand for decoration. Modernism became popular again in the late twentieth century. The appeal of clean lines, custom-designed storage for a clutter-free interior, and open-plan design for relaxed living, is once again returning to the fore.

The color palette

Painted walls are the preferred choice in Modern homes, making for easy change. However, colors are often a combination of neutrals and clear hues, used together or set against clean white.

Lime: A light-reflective, clean, clear color that is surprisingly easy to live with.

Tangerine: A gloriously rich color that should be used only as an accent.

Beige: An elegant shade that looks good on its own, or as a foil both to pastels and brights.

Zinc: A blue gray that sets off clean lines and appears to create shadows and accentuate the form.

Purple: A rich, strong shade that works well on a focus wall in an otherwise white room.

Pebble: A sophisticated soft gray that can be used with other neutrals, or to offset the brights.

▲ **Light and space**
Plenty of natural light pours through large, paned windows to increase the drama of this Modern space composed of asymmetric walls supported by slim, elegant pillars. There is little in the way of decorative embellishment, but the overall effect is one of fascinating layering.

The absence of crown moldings, casings, baseboards, and any other trimwork give Modern interiors a clean, sleek look.

Recessed lighting floods the space, yet leaves the ceiling streamlined.

Floor-to-ceiling windows bathe the room in natural light, a Modern architectural priority. These steel-framed windows are given extra interest with a screening detail.

The bold asymmetrical wall cleverly divides the space, offering drama and dynamism.

A cool slate-tone stucco finish that needs little maintenance.

A simple metal handrail follows through the sleek, unfussy look.

Hard-wearing lumber makes for durable floors.

▲ Smooth operator

Clean, unembellished lines are the hallmark of Modern style. Here, an open-plan space has been divided to create a feeling of space and light.

THE ESSENCE OF MODERN STYLE

Open plan, light filled, and uncluttered, Modern homes are designed for flexible, easy living. Their clean lines smooth out dust-trapping decoration and space-wasting nooks and crannies. Every spare inch is put to good use, providing well-planned storage for speedy and efficient cleanup. Unsightly pipes and electric cables are concealed behind panels or within conduits. Floors are more likely to be finished in easy-to-maintain wood, stone, or ceramic than dust-trapping, wall-to-wall carpeting. Versatile paint for walls eclipses labor-intensive wallpaper, and the more innovative designs incorporate color within the plaster, dispensing with a final finish altogether. Natural light plays a major part, introduced by roof lights, internal windows, glazed doors, and walls of glass blocks.

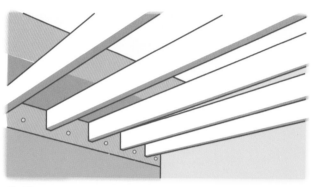

Ceilings

Modern ceilings are either flush and fitted with recessed lighting, or they are "expressed," as here, showing rather than concealing the construction.

▲ Visual tricks

Although Modern style dispenses with trimwork in general, these interiors are by no means uninteresting. Shadow gaps between wall and ceiling make a clean finish, and, in some cases, the wall is detached from the ceiling altogether, as demonstrated by the one carrying the blue painting. Sleek hole-in-the-wall "fireplaces" are typical Modern style.

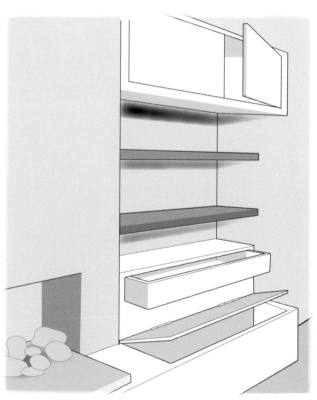

Storage

Flush doors disguise ample storage, appearing to be part of the wall. This arrangement makes use of overhead, under-shelf, and under-bench space.

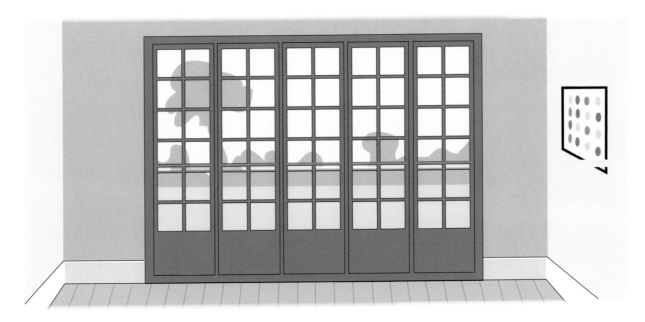

Windows

The key is to have as many windows as possible. Patio doors—folding or sliding versions are popular in Modern homes—are often a priority when remodeling Victorian row houses. Large areas of plate glass are popular, too.

Internal windows

The quest for spaces bathed in natural light inspires Modern homes to use "borrowed" light by creating internal windows to brighten the inner parts of the house.

Staircases

This elegant, sweeping staircase of 1935 with its polished wood handrail and inclined metal balusters, is an example of the Modern Movement departure from traditional upright balusters and newel posts.

DETAIL
DIRECTORY

MAKING DECISIONS

Many architectural embellishments run throughout the house: the style of doors, windows, baseboards, crown moldings, door and window hardware, and even radiators. They don't have to be the same throughout; indeed, it is sometimes not correct for them to be. However, if they are neither matching nor complementary, your home is in danger of looking muddled. These are the embellishments covered in this chapter, cataloged and illustrated to help you. This is not an exhaustive list; it is a taster that provides an outline of the various styles and names associated with buildings of different periods. Whether you are buying "off the shelf" or having embellishments custom-made (see page 14), invest in all you need at one time, even if you have to store part of the order until it's needed. It's more economical that way, and it will all match when the house is fully refurbished.

▲ Traditional glory
Elegant carved marble fireplaces, intricate plaster cornices, and generous casings and baseboards are all hallmarks of elegant period homes.

▶ Clean simplicity
Modern details emphasize sleek lines: flush ceilings with recessed lighting, insignificant or even absent baseboards, and extensive windows with narrow frames.

BASEBOARDS & CHAIR RAILS

The lower parts of walls take the most beating. Indeed, the term chair rail, sometimes called dado rail, hints at their original purpose of protecting the walls against the damage of pulled-back chairs. In many period homes, the chair rail makes an ideal border, below which the walls can be decorated with more substantial finishes, such as wood paneling, tongue and groove board, heavy-duty wallpaper, or a finish of high-gloss paint. The baseboard at the join between the floor and wall provides a cover for that join and hard-wearing protection where the wall is most vulnerable. In period homes, the depth of the baseboard is a common indicator of the quality of the building: the deeper the baseboards, the better the building. Twentieth-century buildings generally have narrower baseboards, and in many modern houses there are no baseboards at all.

▲ Elegant proportion
Chair rails are positioned just where the wall endures the most abuse from chair backs. They also bring a decorative feature to the room.

Chair rails

Convex
Convex chair rails are a good choice for houses with convex baseboards such as torus or ovolo (see opposite).

Concave
Concave chair rails team well with concave moldings, such as ogee.

Bolection
Bolection is a deep, convex molding that is a favorite on paneled Colonial doors, but it is best recognized in its many fireplace applications, especially around the firebox where it houses tiles.

Baseboards

Ovolo
The ovolo molding at the top of this baseboard is inspired by Classical Greek and Roman architecture. The name derives from the seventeenth-century Italian word for "little egg."

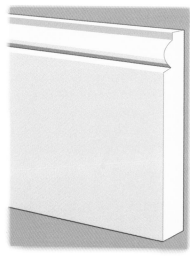

Torus
Torus is a large convex molding that was often found at the base of Greek or Roman columns. It is a popular choice for many period houses.

Victorian
The smooth lines of this Victorian-style baseboard bring an elegant finish to the room.

Regency
This intricate molding is typical of the Regency period in Britain, which influenced the Federal style in America.

Splayed
Splayed baseboards have a simplicity in style that was popular in the mid-twentieth century.

Rounded
Rounded baseboards are without embellishment and ideally suited to modern homes.

PICTURE RAILS & CASINGS

Running around door and window frames, casings provide detail that hugely influences the interior architecture of all houses. The same casings should be specified throughout the house, though in period homes where the middle-level floors are grander than the walk-in and attic levels, simpler versions can be fitted where appropriate. Picture rails, now often referred to as picture moldings, ran around the walls at high level of the grander rooms to accommodate the large hooks from which paintings were hung. Nowadays, pictures are generally hung on hooks fixed into the walls, dispensing with the need for picture rails. Although no longer absolutely needed, it's always advisable to replace picture rails where they have been damaged in period homes as they form part of the architecture of the room.

▲ Elegant detail
Exquisite and restrained, these arched casings add elegance to an octagonal lobby.

Picture rails

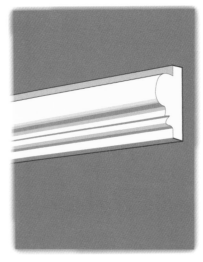

Rounded
The rounded profile of this classic picture rail makes a functional and beautiful solution to hanging paintings without damaging the walls.

Ovolo
This crisp ovolo picture rail brings interest to the upper part of the walls while providing the necessary hanging solution.

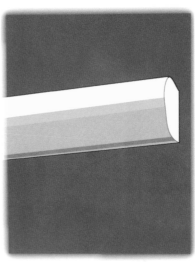

Splayed
Splayed picture rails have a modern feel, and although this may not be purist architecture, the eclecticism of the late twentieth century embraced the addition of details such as picture rails within simple houses.

Casings

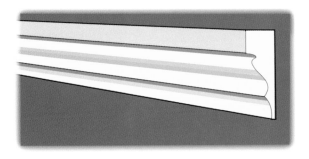

Ogee

Ogee casings were popular throughout the seventeenth to nineteenth centuries. Ogee moldings are those that have an end profile in the shape of a letter. In the case of window and door surrounds, this is always the letter S.

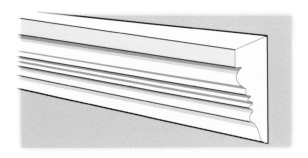

Federal

Classy, reeded-style casings were popular in Federal houses during the early nineteenth century. Instead of mitered corners like most other surrounds, the fashion used blocks or roundels at the corners of doors and windows.

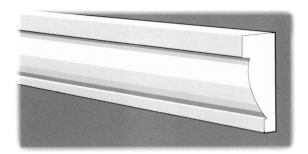

Ovolo

Ovolo casings team well with ovolo baseboards and other moldings, providing a cohesive look to the detailing throughout the house.

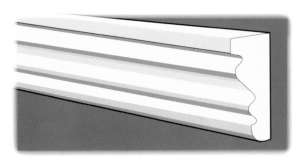

Late nineteenth century

Late nineteenth-century window and door casings took on a more decorated and feminine look, forsaking the Federal looks derived from Roman army decoration.

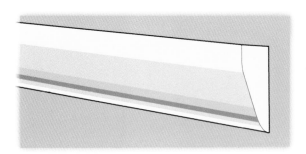

Splayed and rounded

Splayed and rounded surrounds were the no-nonsense choice for late twentieth-century homes.

Federal

Elegant Federal-style moldings provide handsome framing for doors and windows.

CEILING MOLDINGS

The elegant high ceilings of many period houses were decorated with lavish plaster detail. Along with crown moldings and cornice friezes, there were ceiling medallions, corbels, and plaster blocks, as well as fine plaster moldings used to decorate the whole ceiling with ornate designs. Ready-made reproductions are still available—often in wood or synthetics—but nothing can replicate the skills of a restoration plasterer who can reproduce any molding, even matching damaged details in period houses. By cutting out a small sliver of the molding to reveal the full profile, the plaster craftsman can make a mold to run off any length of replacement.

▲ Full suite
Decorative corbels like this can be made from plaster or wood. In the eighteenth and nineteenth centuries, many had detailing inspired by Greek and Roman Classical architecture, featuring acanthus leaves, fruit, and scrolls.

Ceiling medallions

Simple
Unembellished concentric moldings make for elegant, understated ceiling medallions that perfectly complement the Colonial style.

Federal
The crisp lines of this finely molded medallion are typical of Federal style. The molding has a shallower relief than its predecessor, the Colonial style.

Acanthus
The acanthus leaves in the center of this medallion are a regular motif in period houses, inspired by those found on Classical Greek and Roman columns.

Crown moldings and cornices

Concave crown moldings can either be used on their own, or as an excellent anchor for more elaborate adjoining moldings and friezes on both the walls and ceilings to create a cornice of striking composition.

The convex profile is less common than concave, but equally elegant. Damaged crown moldings can be reproduced to any length, so long as a full profile sliver can be cut from the molding.

Egg and dart is a classic molding consisting of the unlikely combination of egg shapes interspersed with darts.

Classic Greek designs, such as this simple Doric form, were popular in the eighteenth and early nineteenth centuries. This design was a typical Federal-style detail.

Elaborate, Federal-style cornices often combined the cornice with a frieze made up of several layers of designs, sometimes even adding small plaster brackets.

These panel molds, inspired by the famed architect Robert Adam, can be ordered to length, then used to make up ceiling designs of concentric panels around the central medallion.

DETAIL DIRECTORY

CEILINGS

Uninterrupted by furniture, pictures, and accessories, ceilings make the perfect blank canvas for embellishment. Bringing the eye upward, decorated ceilings accentuate the loftiness, creating a lighter feel in the room. Elegant period houses generally had molded plaster ceilings, and the finest were very intricate indeed, while the few Modern ceilings that are molded tend to be simpler, geometric designs. Exposed rafters in houses both old and new can add decorative effect to the space, while beaded board paneling can attractively conceal the ever increasing web of services. Oddly, completely plain ceilings can be overbearing because they present a large blank area. Adding a simple crown molding to even the lowest of ceilings adds a sense of height and lifts the look of the whole room.

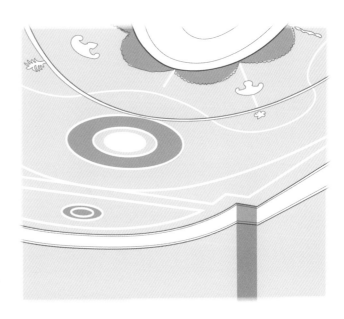

After Adam

Ceilings decorated with intricate moldings in white set against sugar pastel shades were made popular by the Scottish architect Robert Adam, at the end of the eighteenth century.

▲ Modern geometrics

Large-scale geometric moldings add interest to the ceiling of this Modern room painted in white. Although the ceiling is not high, the molding breaks up what is a large surface, providing a lighter feel than if it had been left plain.

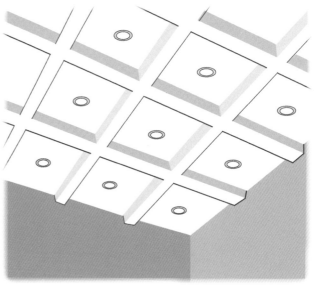

New dimensions

This Modern ceiling has been divided into equal squares by deep moldings, successfully adding interest to the whole space while giving added structure to the lighting positions which become integral to the design.

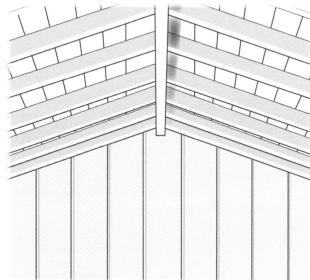

Great combinations

Friezes are often made up of a combination of motifs. Here, reeded sections with corner roundels sit parallel with egg and dart details, forming an unlikely, but successful, combination.

Exposed rafters

The exposed rafters of beach houses and country cottages can make a truly charming design statement. Here, they are painted white to introduce more light to the interior.

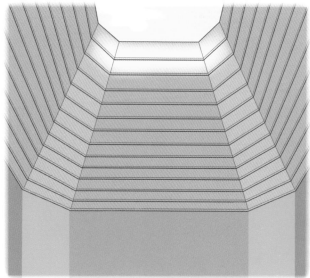

Full exposure

These exposed parallel beams make an exciting design statement with an evocative natural feel in a Modern corridor. They successfully combine the use of natural materials with a functional living area.

Smooth operator

Tongue and groove boards are a useful and versatile material for cladding ceilings, as on this conical roof. Just as effective on a flat ceiling, the wood adds interest, and can be treated with liming wax, stained, or painted.

DOORS

Doors provide a style link that runs throughout the house, so choosing them is key to the overall architecture. As well as the actual door, you need to think about the door casings and trimwork (see page 55) and hardware (see pages 64–65) as both can make a huge difference to the overall finished look. In contemporary homes, the doors are usually a uniform size throughout the house, except where you may have sliding doors for flexible spaces or double doors between rooms. In period houses, on the other hand, it is not unusual to have doors of a similar style throughout the house, but with smaller proportions on the uppermost floors, where the rooms are often smaller and ceiling heights lower.

Sliding doors

These sliding doors are the key to flexible space. Open most of the time, they can quickly be closed to shut away kitchen clutter and create an intimate dining area.

▲ Fresh appeal

This delightful door of beaded board makes a charming choice in a modern Swedish-style country house, perfectly complementing the wood-clad walls painted aqua.

Cool classic

Louvered doors are the classic Caribbean or Southern choice, where there is a need for cool air flow. This is the perfect option for a Plantation-style house.

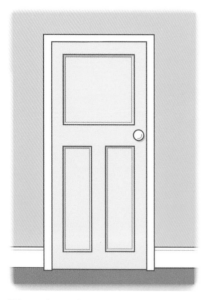

Twenties trio
A single top panel and two lower panels are the typical door style for smaller houses of the 1920s. It was usually teamed with unembellished, unpretentious door surrounds.

Spanish style
Traditional Spanish doors are made from solid wood, often strikingly carved. In period buildings, the hardware is usually forged from handsome wrought iron.

Georgian confidence
Inspired by Classical architecture, Georgian and Federal doors were beautifully proportioned. Always paneled, the larger ones were crowned by pediments.

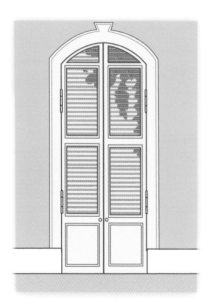

It's a breeze
Cool breezes can filter through the louvers of these Caribbean doors. Finished with a smooth, arched casing, they embody bygone elegance.

Cottage charm
Here is a simple beaded board in natural wood with wrought-iron strap hinges and a thumb latch. It is a cottage classic.

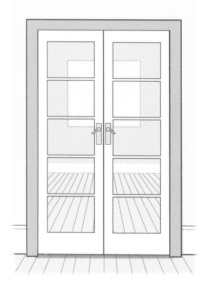

Traveling light
Glazed or part-glazed doors allow light to pass between rooms. This simple pair have flat, natural wood surrounds.

WINDOWS

Although it's best to keep to a window style that is sympathetic to the architecture of the house, this does not necessarily mean all the windows have to be exactly the same. Indeed, most houses are designed with a variety of windows to suit both the exterior elevation and interior needs. If you are buying an old house, the key is to check that the windows are original. The trend in replacement windows toward the end of the twentieth century favored easy-to-maintain, but clumsily designed units. Heavier frames and sashes, especially when installed over existing framework, have a deleterious effect on both the interior and exterior architecture while reducing the amount of light that enters the house. If you wish to restore windows that are closer to the original, start by looking at similar houses, noting the number, configuration, and thickness of the muntins and window frames. This can be a guide for the manufacturer of the new windows.

Victorian bay sash

Bay windows became popular in Victorian times, with windows wider than their Georgian predecessors. There was also more variation in the number of glass panes, ranging from one-over-one, such as this design, to various other, more complex, configurations.

▲ Small perfection

This delightful wood-framed window with its curved top, set in a double recess, has become a focal feature of the room with the added ceramic pots.

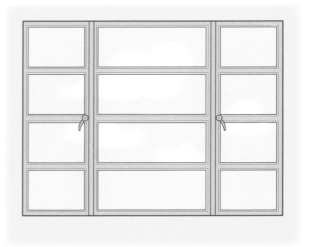

Modern metal

Metal-framed windows became popular in the 1930s. This rectilinear design featuring different-sized panes was first introduced in France, but was soon adopted in America.

Georgian sash

Typical Georgian sash windows had six-over-six panes and fold-back interior shutters, essential for privacy, heat control, and as a block to bright light. The shutters were often paneled in cold climates and louvered in the tropics.

Louvered casements

Half-louvered casements, such as this, are a popular solution in warm climates. The arched top gives charm both to the interior and exterior of the building.

Casement logic

Both inward and outward opening casement windows have been a popular choice since the eighteenth century, and they continue to be so with contemporary architects.

Curved top windows

These pretty windows appeared in America around the end of the nineteenth century, as part of the Queen Anne revival, harking back to seventeenth-century England.

DOOR & WINDOW HARDWARE

It's with the addition of door and window hardware that you can bring your own sense of style to your home. While there are certain types that are correct within an architectural style, there is room for flexibility. For example, door knobs were popular in Victorian times, but you could choose white china for a restrained, elegant feel, or embellished shiny brass for a more sophisticated look. Similarly, both lever handles and knobs were popular in Georgian times. The style you choose for a Federal House comes down to your own particular taste.

Wrought-iron lever
Reminiscent of the blacksmith's work of yore, wrought-iron door fixtures are best restricted to Colonial- and Spanish-style houses, or simple country cottages.

Delicate detail
The pretty detail on this wrought-iron casement stay makes it an excellent choice for Colonial-style homes.

▲ **Style confidence**
This generous, wrought-iron door handle is an unlikely choice in what is a very sophisticated apartment, but the owner has a sureness of style that works. The secret lies in the slender, elegant curve of the handle, which does not overwhelm the fine lines of the door.

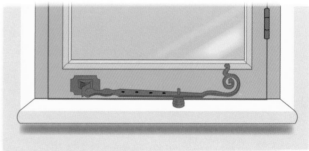

Georgian lever
This centuries-old Classical design is still used for both period houses and contemporary homes.

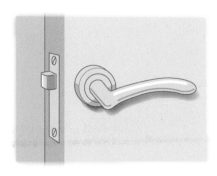

Modern simplicity

Lever handles with smooth lines in stainless steel with polished or satin finishes have become the popular Modern choice.

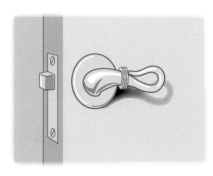

More ornate

A chrome lever handle needn't be a smooth affair; some interiors would benefit from something a little more elaborate, as here.

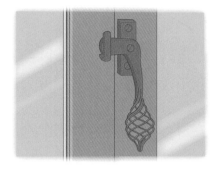

Country style

The scroll end of this wrought-iron casement fastener provides excellent grip: its style is the perfect choice for any country home.

China smoothness

White china or wooden knobs were the Victorian favorite for simpler houses. Their clean lines also work in Modern homes.

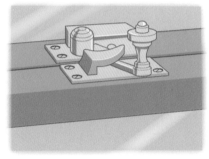

Swing time

This Victorian sash fastener swings across from one window to the next to lock the sashes into position when they are closed.

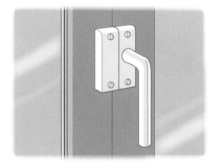

Functional form

Modern casement fasteners are practical and fuss free and designed to be functional rather than decorative.

Brass knobs

Plain or molded brass knobs were used in grander homes in the eighteenth and nineteenth centuries.

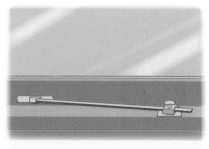

Smart brass

This brass casement stay with a neat thumb-turn fastening would suit any twentieth-century house.

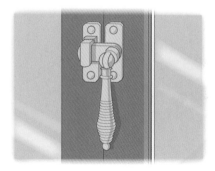

Pretty lovely

Unobtrusive yet tactile, this Victorian brass casement fastener is a pleasure to use.

HARD FLOORS

Beautiful and lasting, hard flooring should be seen more as a permanent fixture than as a fashion choice as it is invariably expensive to supply and lay. Retaining or restoring the original floor is usually the best solution as it will most suit the architecture. If this is not possible, aim to replace it with a material that is used locally in houses of the same period, which will put the building in the context of its surroundings.

Stone

Smooth, hard wearing, and cool, stone is an enduring flooring choice throughout houses in warmer climates, while local limestone flagstones and slates are traditionally used on the ground floor.

◆ **Marble and granite** are the hardest of stones, having been formed under immense pressure and heat deep within the Earth's crust. This makes them hard wearing,

▲ **Wood alternatives**
White-painted floorboards are a typical Swedish detail that has become popular in recent years. The floorboards should be painted using special, hard-wearing floor paint.

water resistant, heatproof, and easy to keep clean.
◆ **Limestone** is a sedimentary stone, formed over millions of years from the skeletons of tiny marine animals. Available in sandy tones, grays, and browns, it is highly porous and less resilient than marble or granite, so it requires a protective finish before use.
◆ **Slate** is attractive and very durable, with a natural riven surface. It is available in grays and dark greens, blues, and browns.

Clay tiles and brick

Made from local baked clay rather than quarried stone, these are a popular floor material the world over as they are easier to handle and transport than stone. Their appeal is their glorious natural color and finish, which is resilient and easy to maintain.

◆ **Clay tiles** are available in various shapes, such as hexagons, lozenges, triangles, and squares, which can be laid to create interesting effects. They are sometimes enhanced with a glossy wax, which gives depth to the color and provides protection. However, the wax does need regular polishing and occasional reapplication.
◆ **Bricks** are also made from clay, but in different-shaped molds. They can be laid in brick-bond fashion or herringbone to create different patterns.
◆ **Encaustic tiles** come in various natural earth tones, which are created by adding pigment to the clay prior to baking.

Glazed ceramics

Waterproof and resilient, glazed ceramic tiles offer endless design choices that range from highly colored and patterned to imitation stone, such as limestone effect.
◆ **Glazed ceramic tiles** can vary in size and shape from tiny mosaics to huge stone-like slabs. They can be square, oblong, hexagonal, round, or even shaped like random pebbles.
◆ **The glaze** can be high gloss or matte and color choice is seemingly limitless. They can also be decorated

before firing. Mediterranean people have painted theirs by hand in intricate designs since pre-Roman times, though they are now more likely to be printed.

◆ **Grout color** and the way in which glazed ceramics are laid add yet more design dimensions.

Wood

For warmth, comfort, and its natural good looks, wood retains lasting appeal. However, it is not nearly as resilient as stone and ceramic, and doesn't take too kindly to stiletto heels or the dragging of furniture. If the surface is damaged, it can be sanded and resealed.

◆ **The wide variety in wood grain** pattern and tone ranges from the palest birch and creamy maple to deep-est walnut with mid-toned oak and elm and rich pink-brown cherry between.

◆ **Wood** can be supplied as boards up to six inches wide and more, strip flooring with boards composed of several narrow pieces, and parquet blocks of small strips laid mosaic fashion onto square base tiles. It is also possible to have inlaid wood, supplied as ready-made medallion and border pieces to be put together on-site, or completely craftsman-made on-site.

◆ **Wood can be stained,** which penetrates and dyes the timber, varnished, which puts a protective layer on top; waxed or oiled, both of which protect the wood. Another option is to paint the floor with special hard-wearing floor paint.

Lasting style

Little matches the beauty of a stone floor, worn to link the house with the very ground on which it stands.

Falling into shape

These curvy tiles lend an attractive pattern to a Mediterranean-style floor.

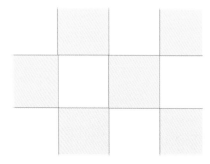

Checkerboard pattern

Glazed ceramics are an excellent traditional flooring for hallways because of their durability.

Natural color

Tessellated floors made from pigmented encaustic tiles are traditional to Victorian buildings. Subtle mosaics of geometric shapes, they were often used for halls.

Pattern perfection

Wood provides plenty of scope for pattern. The main part of this floor has been laid parquet-style while the oak-leaf border came ready-made and was cut to fit.

RESILIENT & SOFT FLOORS

While solid floors can be expected to last a building's lifetime, it is not unusual to change softer floors within five years, which allows much more versatility in terms of design trends. Both resilient and soft flooring offer a much wider choice of colors and patterns. Deep-pile floor coverings, such as wool carpets, also provide insulation against noise and heat loss.

Resilient flooring

◆ **Available in sheet or tile form,** most resilient flooring is less expensive than hard flooring.

◆ **Vinyl cushion flooring** is inexpensive, easy for the layman to cut and lay and available in myriad patterns and colors.

◆ **Top-quality hard vinyl tiles** come in many innovative designs, but they are almost as expensive as ceramic and require professional laying.

◆ **Rubber floors** are stylish, durable, and fashionable, and can be supplied in a vast array of colors. Choose from a smooth surface or an excellent selection of studs and textures.

◆ **Linoleum** is a natural product made from linseed oil, resins, cork, ground limestone, and wood dust. It was popular in Victorian days, but lost its reputation to vinyl in the second half of the twentieth century. Now available in fashionable colors, it is seeing a revival.

Vinyl life

Sheet vinyl flooring designs very often imitate glazed ceramic tiles and other more ornate patterns, though there is now a much larger choice of plain styles available together with wood effects.

▲ Soft option

Attractive and soft underfoot, wall-to-wall carpet is a sophisticated, luxurious floor choice for bedrooms. Here, the same carpet is used throughout the upper floor for an elegant, cohesive look.

Pattern today

This elegant taupe and cream geometric design is more restrained than a traditional patterned carpet and so creates a stylish living room carpet that would be perfect for a Modern home.

Carpet

Wall-to-wall carpeting was a popular twentieth-century choice, especially in northern climates, giving insulation that kept the heat in and noise out. Despite the revival of hardwood floors and ceramic tiles, a desire remains for the comfort of bedrooms with carpets underfoot.

◆ **Fiber content** is a major consideration when buying. Wool is the luxury end of the carpet market as it provides excellent body and resists stains. A mix of 80% wool and 20% synthetic for extra resilience is the most popular choice. Acrylic is the synthetic closest to wool, though it is more inclined to show stains. Nylon is tough, but flattens with time, and attracts more stains. Polyester is a soft fiber most often associated with shag-pile carpets, though it must be woven into a very dense pile to avoid flattening. Polypropylene and viscose are hard wearing, and used to beef up other fibers.

◆ **Pile** has a bearing on both the durability and the feel of the carpet. Tufted and twisted piles are durable and good looking—a good all-round choice. Velvet is a densely woven short pile, a high-end product that is hard wearing. Looped is the term used when the pile has not been cut. Strong and the least likely to flatten, the surface is prone to matting.

◆ **Weave** affects both the pile and design. Axminsters are woven into the backing from above, which allows for the use of many colors. Wiltons are woven from a single strand of yarn, resulting in densely woven, high-quality carpets of one color. Brussels weave is an uncut looped pile, generally from fiber with a high wool content.

Natural fibers

Until recently, natural fibers, such as coir, took a backstage role and were used mainly as carpet backing. However, with their versatile natural tones and hard-wearing quality, they have become a popular choice for floor coverings. With a wide array of weaves available, such as basket weave and herringbone, they can bring glorious texture to the floor. The stiffness of the fiber and natural tendency to stretch once they are laid means they are more difficult than traditional carpets to install. However, once down, they are hard wearing and resilient, with a natural tendency to repel stains.

◆ **Coir** is the fiber traditionally used for floor mats. Sturdy and textured, it is ideal for heavy traffic areas.

◆ **Sisal** has similar qualities to coir, but is softer and finer for a more elegant end result.

◆ **Jute** is the softest of the naturals, ideal for bedrooms.

◆ **Sea grass** is slippery, so is not suitable for stairs. It is inclined to break up, and is best used in less formal situations, such as enclosed porches.

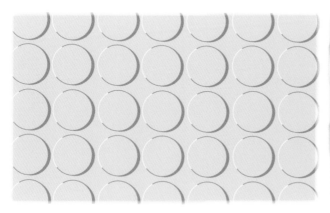

Rainbow choices
Rubber flooring can be supplied in as many colors as paint. It needs to be fitted professionally with the factory finish stripped off before a protective finish can be applied.

Texture treat
The handsome herringbone weave of this jute carpeting is accentuated with a contrast weft, adding a strong textural element to the room.

RADIATORS & COVERS

Warming cold spaces without the bother of building open fires, radiators have contributed greatly to the comfort of rooms in cold climates. However, until recently they have been the stepchild of the interior, so designers have traditionally gone to great lengths to cover them up. This simply reduces their effectiveness, say the heating engineers, who, after more than a century, are at last confronting the issue and designing interesting radiators that look less like a piece of machinery and more like a sculpture. If you have inherited plain, bulky radiators that you hate, then cover them up; if you want to change your radiators, look at some of the newer ones that can be worked into your interior design. Period houses that are having their floors replaced may be better off dispensing with radiators altogether and opting for underfloor heating.

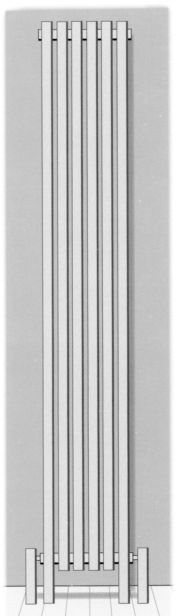

Shiny style
Sleek square tubes in shiny chrome create a very chic radiator that can be as tall and thin or low and wide as you like. Matching valves, also clad in shiny chrome, put this radiator ahead of the game.

▲ Heavily disguised
Radiators can be very ugly objects in any room, but especially in a bedroom. A practical option is to cover the radiator with a grille, which immediately makes the area look more attractive and can make for a useful shelf, too.

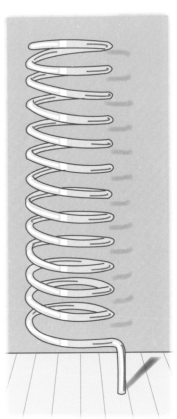

Hot spring
Giant springs, like this, can be installed vertically or horizontally to suit the architecture.

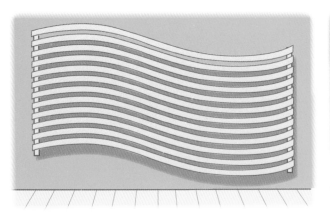

Curvy lines

Modern flat-panel radiators are beginning to take on curves, becoming wall sculptures that no longer need covering up.

Efficient cover

White covers of medium density fiberboard (MDF) with anodized aluminum grilles offer an efficient way to cover up less than beautiful radiators.

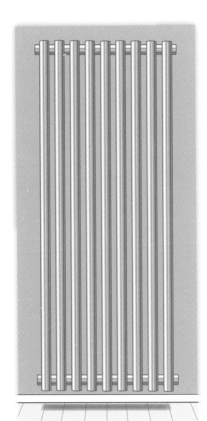

Tubular column

Parallel tubes, made to any length and stacked to any width, make this an elegant, versatile radiator.

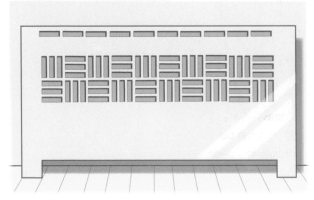

Wooden style

Natural wooden radiator covers, such as this, would make an excellent solution in period houses between 1870 and 1930.

Metal guru

Stainless steel covers not only look great, they are excellent conductors of heat and so restrict the heat output less than other radiator covers.

ROOM
BY ROOM

PRIORITIES

Although many architectural embellishments run right through the house, each room also has different priorities that are, first and foremost, practical but that can also be historic. These historic priorities may or may not have changed over the years, and, depending on the period of your house, this may affect your choice. The following chapter looks at these issues and outlines your options for embellishments that are particularly important in each area of the house. It's best to decide on these after, not before, you've chosen the details that run through the house. You can then be sure the embellishments that are particular to each room sit well with the rest of the house.

▲ Federal classic
Living rooms are the showcase of the house, often displaying the finest of architectural detail. Here, the elegantly detailed fireplace, fine crown molding and architrave, and built-in shelves are all classic Federal style, giving the room tremendous unity.

▶ Original charm
The floors in halls need to be the most hard wearing in the house and are usually chosen for their lasting quality. The large carved wooden door and clay-tiled floor are probably original to the house, and over the years they have withstood much wear and tear.

LIVING & DINING ROOMS

relaxed

display

elaborate

minimal

elegant

grand

fireplaces

lighting

open plan

cozy

LIVING & DINING ROOMS

SHOWCASE DETAILS

Living and dining rooms, where the family spends most of its time and where guests are entertained, are the showrooms of the house. Indeed, in many traditional houses, a special room is set aside from the commotion of family life, and kept clean and tidy specifically for the entertainment of guests. This is where architects and builders specify the very best of details. In period houses, crown moldings, picture rails, wainscoting, and trimwork are at their most elaborate and doors and windows their most generous. Where living and dining rooms are linked by double doors, the openings will often be elaborately embellished with moldings. But it is the ceilings that are most often the *pièce de résistance* of grand parlors and reception rooms. They often have elaborate plaster cornices and friezes, and in some houses, the plaster work is extended right across the ceiling in beautiful geometric or concentric designs around an elaborate ceiling medallion.

The eighteenth-century Scottish architect Robert Adam designed triumphant ceilings that featured flowers, fruits, garlands, even maidens' profiles, and painted them in his signature palette of clear pastels. His influence stretched across the Atlantic and endured for more than a century, making its mark especially in Federal houses. Today's casual lifestyles mean that special rooms are rarely set aside exclusively for entertaining, but the main living spaces are still endowed with the very best of detailing.

▶ Pretty in panels

The delightful proportions of this Colonial living room are complemented by floor-to-ceiling windows and subtle molding on the walls. Painted pink and white, the room has all the refined elegance of an eighteenth-century Parisian apartment.

A generous crown molding adds a sense of grandeur and extra height.

Simple casings complement floor-to-ceiling windows, which flood the room with light.

Plaster molding brings interest to the walls. Panels of different sizes help to visually adjust the proportions of the walls.

An unfussy English-style marble mantelpiece is typical of the Colonial style.

Polished wood laid in herringbone fashion brings a quality finish to the floor.

LIVING & DINING ROOMS

▲ Clean Modern

A sleek lack of embellishment is the hallmark of good Modern design. Here, baseboards are kept to the minimum and the trimwork has a flat profile for a clean, simple look aimed at relaxed, easy living.

▲ Light fantastic

Natural light is a modern priority, so here the windows occupy most of one wall, and the muntins are kept as fine as possible. A generous use of wood from the floor to the walls and on the ceiling places the building well in harmony with its forest environment.

◀ **A sense of proportion**

Complemented by floor-to-ceiling windows, an outsize fireplace adds a sense of grandeur to this contemporary room. The mood is carried through with a beamed ceiling.

FIREPLACES

Fireplaces are symbolic of all the home comforts: warmth on a cold winter's night; relaxation at the end of the day; companionship with friends and family. Little wonder, then, that great energy has been expended developing ever more elaborate designs as fireplaces happily occupy the pride of place within the home. In America, Federal-style mantelpieces made grand statements with pilasters, pediments, and plaster decoration.

But with the growth of central heating, fireplaces found that their place in twentieth-century homes had been claimed by TV sets. However, the appeal of the fireplace has proven irresistible, and most contemporary homes are designed to include them. They look different now with clean gas flames dancing around manufactured "coals," "logs," pebbles, and even pyramid shapes, replacing the messier but more evocative roaring log fire. However, this cleanup has liberated design, which ranges from grand architectural statements to sleek hole-in-the-wall and brazier styles that can be placed in the center of the room.

▶ Grand style
Tall chimneypieces became popular during the Federal period and again during the revival of the early twentieth century. Mantelpieces were topped with elaborate pilasters, pediments, and plaster decorations, such as this.

▶▶▲ Neat petite
Sleek hole-in-the-wall fireplaces epitomize Modern style. This slim-line version perfectly complements the narrow chimney breast in which it is set.

▶▶ Smart statement
The sculptural quality of this fireplace is typical of contemporary design, giving a focus to the room. Set off-center on the chimney, its pigmented concrete and metal construction make it stand out against the simple tongue and groove wall.

DECORATIVE LIGHT FIXTURES

Decorative light fixtures, such as hanging lamps and wall sconces, make a big contribution to the overall architecture of living rooms. Since the wires must be hidden behind the walls, this is a decision that needs to be made early on. The original architectural details of the building are a good clue as to what lights you should choose. If you have a fine Colonial house, you could consider pretty wrought-iron lamps, while crystal chandeliers and hanging lamps in the lantern style suit Federal houses. The central lights in houses of the Twenties and Thirties were often suspended on chains with bowl-like shades made from cut or marbled glass. Wall sconces could be made from brass and even Bakelite with Art Deco detailing, or pretty molded glass, often in the form of shells. With the advent of low-voltage halogen, Modern lighting has taken on a completely different look. Generous light can be emitted from tiny fixtures, freeing up the whole area of lighting design.

▲ **Conversion rates**
Original chandeliers can be converted to electrical fixtures, and now many reproductions are made for electricity. Here, glass beads, flowers, and drip trays set against elegant serpentine metal have a charm that would enhance any living or dining room.

◄ Metal style

Wrought-iron candelabras are a familiar American sight from early Colonial times. Their appeal is that they could incorporate a large number of candles yet still retain a lightness of structure. This fixture works well in a lovely feminine dining area, but the unpolished metal would look equally good in a more masculine environment.

◄◄ Drum beat

Restrained drum lampshades, used both on hanging fixtures and for table lights, are an icon of Fifties style. They still look elegant in Modern and contemporary houses.

LIVING & DINING ROOMS
WALL INTEREST

Most wall embellishments are found where the ceiling meets the walls; where the walls meet the floor; or around features, such as doors, windows, or fireplaces. However, in the past, large expanses of ceilings and walls were seen as "canvases" that could be given relief with the addition of molding, plaster motifs, or wood paneling. Contemporary walls are less likely to be embellished in these ways, though molding and wood paneling are still popular. Beaded board, brickwork, and tiles can also be used to make a feature of whole or parts of walls. Modern architecture, which shuns embellishment, brings interest to walls by using shadow gaps between wall and ceiling, or by using a different finish on focus walls, such as plaster that has been polished to a sheen, or concrete.

▲ All white

Even the simplest panels make a feature of prominent walls. Here, the whole space has been painted white to create a light, airy effect, but with the textural relief of the paneled wall.

▲ Pretty features

Here, the wall panels have been embellished with exquisite Adam-style plaster garlands to give the effect of huge picture frames.

◀ Tile style

Pretty tiles add decorative interest to the wall while providing protection to the lower part, which takes the hardest knocks.

◀◀ Feature bricks

The brick-faced chimney in this Modern room makes a feature of the fireplace by providing a contrast in texture, which is accentuated by painting it white to match the rest of the room.

FLOOR TREATMENTS

The flooring needs of living and dining rooms can be quite different. In living rooms the priority is relaxed comfort, while spill-prone activities in the dining room mean easy cleanup becomes more of a priority. This is no problem when the rooms are separate: the challenge comes with open-plan living. The classic solution is to use a change of flooring material to delineate the space for the different activities, perhaps by installing hard floors throughout and then adding generous rugs to the living area. As an alternative, carpet can be laid atop hard flooring, neatened by wood or metal threshold rods.

You first need to consider the overall look you're after. Do you love a sleek wall-to-wall look, or would you prefer to create a visual boundary between the two different areas? Even if you are using different materials, both are possible by working with tone. If you'd like a coordinated look, choose materials of a similar shade. For a strong demarcation between the living and dining areas, use materials with great contrast.

▲ Open-plan living

For optimum use of both space and light, open-plan living has much to commend it, but sometimes it can be difficult to make the different areas appear "grounded." Here, the huge shaggy rug brings comfort to the living area and gives it a sense of purpose within the larger space.

▲ Luxury living

Wall-to-wall carpeting is wonderfully soft underfoot for a luxurious feel in the living room. Modern geometric patterns, such as this one, give a dynamism to the floor and can add textural interest, too.

◄ Tonal treat

For an elegant, cohesive look, concentrate on choosing materials with similar tones. This exquisite limestone floor runs wall to wall throughout the space. A large jute rug in the seating area provides comfort and doesn't affect the color scheme.

BUILT-IN STORAGE

Most of us think of built-in storage as a modern innovation, yet it's been part of domestic architecture for centuries. The Shakers designed wonderful floor-to-ceiling units containing drawers and cupboards custom-sized to suit their contents. They made the best use of the space by filling whole walls, which gave ample storage space while excluding dust traps. It's a trick we still need to apply today and particularly when thinking of storage for living and dining rooms. These are the rooms in which we relax and want to display our most beautiful and treasured personal effects, such as family photographs, exquisite vases, and sculptures, but we also want to conceal some of our less beautiful accessories, such as video tapes, CDs, and DVDs. The design of built-in storage probably has the greatest influence on the personality of the room, because it will dictate what we hide and what we put on display. Purist Modern architects would aim to hide everything behind flush closet doors, letting the building itself become a piece of artwork. And although that makes for quick and easy housekeeping, many people prefer to have somewhere to keep those treasured items that express their own personalities. Some built-in furniture comprises both closet and display, making the best of both worlds, while other pieces are distinctly designed for showing things off.

◀ On display

Using the alcoves on either side of a fireplace is a traditional yet highly practical use of space for storage. Here, beautifully shaped casseroles and pretty serving plates create an attractive display on the shelves while glasses are kept below in the glass-fronted cabinets. The shapely carved additions at the top of the shelves make these alcoves even more of a feature within the room.

▲ Great combination

While we want to keep some of our most treasured possessions on display in the living room, other items, such as CDs and DVDs, are best hidden away. Combined systems can provide the best solution, providing closets for the practical but not necessarily beautiful items and shelves or cubbyholes to accommodate family photographs and favorite finds.

KITCHENS

practical

working

meeting place

multifunctional

floors

storage

efficient

entertaining

surfaces

faucets

lighting

FUNCTION FIRST

As the hardest-working room of the house, practicality has to be the priority in the kitchen. This is no place for intricate dust- and grease-trapping embellishments; nooks and crannies are a no-no, and smooth, wipe-clean surfaces are the best time-saving choice. Yet, more and more, this is where families spend most of their time—children do their homework and families dine and entertain friends, so kitchens also need to be light and bright with a welcoming ambience. This can work well, whatever your style: farmhouse kitchens have always been the hub of the home, where families gathered around the stove as much for company as for

▲ Neat solution
Even long, thin kitchens can provide space for both working and relaxing. Here, the breakfast bar extends from the island unit, squeezing a roomy kitchen dining counter from limited space.

▶ Home industry
The juxtaposition of an industrial-style cooking area with squishy sofas is the epitome of today's multifunctional kitchen. The exposed metal beams, stainless-steel backsplash, flue, and hospital-style metal trolley display robust, unfussy detailing that makes for relaxed living.

Recessed halogen spots flood light into the room while fitting flush with the ceiling, which ensures no interruption of the sleek lines.

The basement kitchen is galleried with the ground floor so light can flood in from above.

The metal beams have been expressed to show the structure of the building, bringing interest to the architecture.

Flush-fronted cupboards have concealed hinges and a push-open, push-shut mechanism requiring no handles for a contemporary finish.

The terrazzo floor gives a clean uniformity to the space and has the added advantage of housing underfloor heating.

warmth. In grander period houses, the kitchens were servants' territory, a space for living as well as working, in much the same way as kitchens are today.

Kitchens have never been endowed with anything more than plain millwork. Instead, architectural energies are concentrated on efficient storage with the decorative addition of interesting handles, and efficient floors, wall, and work surfaces. Kitchens were the first rooms to universally embrace Modern architecture, partly because they naturally reflected the ethos of the machine age. In traditional row houses, original cooking spaces were often remodelled in the second half of the twentieth century. They were transformed into places of efficiency, thanks to space-planning lessons learned from fitting out the galley kitchens of ocean liners. In our era, though, space is being reallocated within the house. The result is a new look that sometimes reflects the farmhouse kitchens of old, like island units replacing kitchen tables. When it comes to detail, even in elaborate homes, today's kitchen is most likely to be the sleekest room in the house.

▲▶ Smooth operator

Smooth lines are a priority in modern kitchens. Flush-cupboard doors are free of grease-trapping embellishments such as molding and, in some cases, even the more practical elements, such as handles. With everything put away, wiping down is a breeze.

◀ Tight fit

Fully equipped kitchens like this originally borrowed ideas from the space-planning theories of ships' galley kitchens, resulting in the highly efficient use of space. Not only do they offer maximum storage for many pieces of equipment, they are also effective work spaces.

▲ In style

The molded cupboard doors, Victorian-style faucets and turned legs of the island unit reflect the overall style of this restored nineteenth-century house. However, efficient kitchen planning ensures that the cupboards make the best use of available space.

WALLS

The daily deluge of steam, water splashes, grease, and airborne grime demands that kitchen walls are water resistant. Interestingly, this means that there are more, rather than fewer, choices of finish. Beside paint (choose wipe-clean eggshell paint, rather than a more absorbent matte finish), there's a choice of ceramic, stainless steel panels, beaded board with glossy paint, tiles, glass tiles, colored sheet glass, and even glass bricks. These finishes can be used throughout the kitchen, but more often they are preferred for the wet and cooking areas and around the sink. The rest of the room can be treated quite differently. Add the fact that much of the wall area is occupied by cupboard or shelf space, and we find that a variety of materials and finishes can be cleverly mixed, making the walls in the kitchen the most interesting in the house.

▲ Cool combination

Resilient eggshell paint has been applied to the beaded board splashback and all the kitchen units for an allover cool look, complementing the duck egg-blue lower units.

◄◄▲ Two-tone treat
Burnt orange paint gives an intensity to this kitchen furnished with simple beech cupboards. The classic units were chosen because they transcend time while the walls are treated to extravagant color that can be updated as fashions change.

◄ Pretty but practical
Ceramic tiles have proved their worth over more than two millennia. Since Roman times they've brought a decorative touch to wet surfaces. Here, plain blue and printed blue tiles have been arranged to create interesting diamond patterns in an otherwise all-white kitchen.

◄◄▼ Light fantastic
Stainless steel is a handsome and modern kitchen material, reflecting plenty of light for a bright, new look. While it wipes clean without effort, it is, however, quite susceptible to scratches.

KITCHEN FLOORS

Hard wearing and easy to clean—these are the priorities for kitchen flooring. Traditional stone floors and glazed ceramic tiles measure up on both requirements and have certainly stood the test of time. The floors of some ancient houses, uncovered during archaeological digs in Europe, are often still intact after hundreds of years. But both of these are hard underfoot and any china or glass dropped on them will shatter in an instant. They are also expensive to buy and install. A slightly softer traditional option is wood—although the drawback to wood is that it easily dents and damages if knives and pans are dropped on it. In the last hundred years, more resilient materials have emerged, including rubber and vinyl. Of these, vinyl is the most economical both to buy and to lay as this can be tackled by the layman (see also pages 68–69).

▲ Cool ceramic tile
Ceramic tiles provide one of the most resilient, impervious surfaces available, having been baked at an extremely high temperature. Available in every conceivable color, these white tiles with gray grout and black inserts are a cool, Modern choice.

▶ Stunning stone
Limestone coated with a protective finish matches the pale wood units in a sleek and elegant look that suits contemporary and traditional houses.

▲ Rubber choice

Resilient, easy underfoot, and available in an infinite range of shades, rubber is the almost perfect kitchen floor. However, it is not cheap, and installation can mean two different teams: one to cut and fit, and the next to strip off the factory finish and apply the final coating, which can be expensive. Once down, however, rubber always offers a long-term solution.

◀ Wood for warmth

More forgiving and warmer underfoot than stone, wood is a popular traditional choice in colder climates. However, it is not as resilient as stone and ceramic tiles and will dent under pressure from sharp heels or dragged furniture.

KITCHEN CUPBOARDS

More than any other element, the choice of cupboards will dictate the overall style of the kitchen. Paneled or molded doors generally have a more traditional feel; flush usually looks more contemporary. The way they are used will also influence the final effect.

As a general rule, during the latter half of the twentieth century, whatever the style of the doors, cupboards completely lined the walls of kitchens both large and small. Before then, storage was more likely to be on shelves, or in freestanding cabinets and china closets. Today, Modern kitchens combine the best of both worlds by using the principles of built-in units to create the sleek, uniform look of a furnished room. Island units are a modern form of the traditional farmhouse kitchen table which usually occupied the middle of the room.

▲ Royal flush

Flush doors and drawers and fully fitted units have a sleek, contemporary look. By choosing a wood finish, this kitchen is unlikely to date quickly.

▲ All in the detail

Pretty trimwork and elegant muntins on the glass-fronted cupboards all add up to a style that would be in keeping with an elegant period house. Clever modern planning incorporates them into an efficient kitchen.

◄ All white

Simple paneled doors give a classic feel to these white cupboards. Set within the context of an open living-dining area, the cupboards bring a relaxed domestic feel to a practical area that is in keeping with this interior.

◄◄ Modern efficiency

Simple use of space, with a row of units along one wall plus a central island, is both easy on the eye and offers ample storage. No unnecessary embellishments adorn these sleek, Modern cupboards.

KITCHENS

CUPBOARD HANDLES

Put different handles on the same cupboards, and the kitchen will take on a whole different character. Knobs generally add a traditional feel. Choose from small or large, metal, wood, ceramic, or acrylic. Handles can be small and unassuming, or long, stretching the full width of the drawers. Longer handles generally look more contemporary than shorter styles, though it is worth pointing out that whatever the current fashion, practicality should take precedence over looks. So try them out to check that little parts don't make them hard to use or that they don't have too many crevices to catch spills and grime. Many modern kitchen cupboards are designed to have no handles at all, leaving the doors flush for easy maintenance. On the whole, cupboard doors are generally easier and more convenient to open if the handles are fitted vertically, though if you want a cohesive look, they can be fitted horizontally in line with the drawers.

▲ Barely there

Choosing flush cupboards with no visible handles is as much a design choice in terms of the overall effect as choosing any other kind of handle. Here, the overall look is sleek, yet the cupboards are trimmed with the most discreet metal handles at the corners of the doors.

◀ Neat choice

Metal knobs perfectly complement these paneled drawer and door fronts—the ideal choice for a kitchen set within a period home.

 **Simple solution**
Understated metal handles give a no-nonsense, utilitarian feel to the whole kitchen.

▶ **Long and lean**
Long metal handles emphasize the design of the extrawide drawers, giving the whole kitchen a generous look. Matching handles are fixed vertically on the doors, giving a geometric rhythm to the row of cupboards for a Modern feel.

KITCHEN SURFACES

It's a tall order to expect any surface to be water, heat, and cut and scratch resistant, but those are the qualities an ideal work surface will offer. Granite is the closest you'll ever get to that ideal. Available in many different colors, it offers plenty of design scope, though it is expensive and not suitable as a chopping surface. However, most of us naturally use boards for cutting and chopping and trivets for hot pans, which opens up a much wider choice, including granite, artificial marble, ceramic and stone tiles, wood, and laminates.

Stainless steel, which is traditionally used in professional kitchens, has also become very popular for its clean, light sheen. However, although it is impervious to water and normal food stains, it does scratch easily, and the kitchen-proud can be driven demented, continually polishing off finger marks. Polished concrete is another "new" kitchen work surface that, when prepared properly, is a suitable, wonderfully tough option for contemporary-style homes.

▶ **New horizons**
Polished concrete, such as this, can look very attractive indeed, especially if water-resistant additives and color have been included in the original mix. It looks hard, but it won't take kindly to chopping and cutting.

▼ **Steely light**
Stainless steel brings a fresh look to domestic kitchens. The perfect finish won't last forever: Be prepared for small abrasions and scratches.

KITCHEN FAUCETS

Choosing kitchen faucets comes down to a combination of practicality, the style of your kitchen, and your own personal taste. From a practical standpoint, bear in mind that you'll need to fit pots, pans, and kettles under the spout; so if yours are tall, a high-arch style would be the best choice. Do you prefer separate spouts for hot and cold water or a single lever that mixes them together? Do your plans include a side spray or a soap dispenser? All these decisions will affect how many holes need to be made in the worktop, or, if you have a surface-mounted sink, check that it comes with the correct number of holes.

When choosing the style of your faucets, first bear in mind the style of your kitchen. Sleek, modern faucets with a single lever control may look elegant in a minimalist kitchen, but would be quite out of place in a more traditional-style room fitted with paneled cupboards. In this situation, it would be better to choose fixtures with cross-head turn handles.

◄ **Money no problem**

If budget isn't a restraint, look at the many designer faucets that are available. Made of high-quality materials and sporting unusual taps and shapes, you can buy something very special for your kitchen.

▲ Six-hole solution

An efficient array of faucets and valves line up behind a double-bowl basin in this Modern kitchen. The spout is served by hot and cold levers with a soap dispenser to the left. On the right are a side spray for rinsing and separate cold faucet for washing produce.

▲ Professional solution

Great for state-of-the-art kitchens, this all-in-one unit consists of a spout that doubles as a flexible hose to rinse dishes and produce because you can carefully direct the flow of water.

▲ Love levers

To make life as straightforward as possible, choose a faucet that has levers as a part of its mechanism as these are easy to use when hands are slippery. They make a strong style statement, too.

DECORATIVE LIGHTS

Decorative lighting can bring interesting detail to the kitchen, introducing architectural interest at a high level. Even if recessed fixtures provide most of the background lighting, decorative hanging lights can be used to lend extra focus to particular features. This works especially well if the kitchen is also a dining and living room. Although adding to the architectural style of the kitchen is the main function of decorative lighting, bear practicality in mind, too. Any kitchen will be subject to airborne grease which must be cleaned—a much easier job on smoother, non-absorbent surfaces. From a design standpoint, choose fixtures that add to the style of the kitchen, rather than the period of the house.

▲ Sixties cool

A neat fixture with five drum shades is the perfect Sixties-style choice to hang over the pedestal table and wire chairs from the same period.

▲ Lantern life

Two lines of traditional lanterns make a striking statement in this generous kitchen with period styling. In the dining area beyond, the fine wire chandelier emphasizes a more relaxed space for entertaining.

▶ Pure simplicity

Adjustable hanging lights with glass shades add an elegant touch over a traditional-style kitchen table. This is a clever choice: The design dates from the turn of the twentieth century, yet its clean lines have never dated.

HALLS, LANDINGS & STAIRS

welcome

link

doorways

sweeping

floors

balustrades

handrails

stairs

corbels

archways

UNIQUE OPPORTUNITIES

The foyer or entrance hall is where first impressions count. Like the cover of a book, this is where you are first introduced to the contents. There's the entry hall itself, but in addition, like book jacket notes, there are glimpses into the rooms beyond. Doorways and their trimwork play an important role in connecting spaces, as this is the only area where they become true team players. Most rooms have one, maybe two doorways; when halls and landings are seen as a single space, this can easily multiply to ten or more, so they have a huge influence on the space as a whole.

Together with living rooms, hallways are where architects traditionally concentrate some of the most interesting details. In period houses, hallway cornices are often at their most elaborate, including decorative plaster blocks and elegant corbels, even if they don't appear anywhere else in the house. The stairway itself offers an element unique to halls and landings. Sweeping handrails, serried ranks of balusters, and decorative tread ends all bring decorative detail to this uniquely vertical element of the house.

Often located in the central part of the home, halls can be dark affairs, so in period houses, wall sconces and chandeliers or lanterns play a leading role in the architectural detailing. Light fixtures also contribute to modern halls, but this is a less important element as there is often a greater introduction of natural daylight in the form of skylights, and light levels can be boosted by barely visible recessed lighting of low voltage. From a practical point of view, hallways are high-traffic areas that incur more damage than most other spaces in the house, so there's a need for tough surfaces such as hard floors and resilient walls, and the inherent beauty of both makes a welcoming entrance.

▶ **Sweeping statement**
This winding handrail has been given focus in an elegant hallway by contrasting its smooth lines against the white balusters.

Wood stair treads add elegant detailing to the staircase. This is particularly spectacular where the tread ends contrast with the painted strings, accentuating the sweep of the winding stair.

▲ **Highly polished**
The beautiful original oak floor in this hallway has been polished over the years, building up a glorious patina which cannot be reproduced in a new floor.

Polished wooden floorboards make for a smart entrance that is nevertheless resilient enough to withstand the hardest wear in the house.

High-level intricate plasterwork brings interest to the stairway, which can be appreciated both from the ground and upper levels.

Carpet on the stairs both protects the treads and provides a safe, non-slip surface.

Turned balusters add pretty detail to the stairway. They are often painted white in period houses, giving a light and airy feel to the hall and staircase.

▲ Lovely landing

The paneling on the side of the stairway brings hard-wearing relief to this landing, a look that is echoed in the window shutters.

▶ Lateral thinking

Balustrades don't always have to be vertical. These lateral examples make a strong statement.

HALL FLOORS

This is the most hard-working floor of the whole house. Everyone has to pass through the hall, bringing a little of the outside with him. For this reason, hall floors need to be hard wearing and easy to clean. It is also a good idea to provide generous entrance matting, preferably in a mat well so the initial grit and grime from outside can be shaken off before being trodden into the rest of the hall. Even tiny quantities of grit can eventually affect the finish on almost any floor. The best way to make a successful choice is to look at local houses of the same period as yours whose occupants have not covered the original floors with other materials.

▲ **Bright white**
Ceramic tiles, cleverly laid to create a subtle pattern, create an especially durable hall floor.

◀ **Creative color**
Ceramic tiles are used in hallways the world over, although each country and region has its own unique designs and patterns. This pretty diamond design brings a warm welcome with color and pattern.

◀ Traditional patterns
Tessellated floors like this
are composed of encaustic
tiles of different shapes and
sizes that fit together like a
puzzle to form geometric
patterns in the natural
colors of the clay. They are
a traditional English style,
but were brought over to
both New England and
parts of the Caribbean.

FLOOR TREATMENTS: LANDINGS & STAIRS

Although the hall, stairs, and landings are sometimes fitted with the same flooring throughout, their needs are quite different. While all need to be durable, this is the major priority for the hall as it takes the greatest knocks and is subject to the most debris coming in from outside. But the stone, ceramic, and wood that can be so ideal in the hall are less practical on the stairs, which should offer good traction. Softer flooring, such as carpet runners or wall-to-wall, work better here, protecting the projecting part of the tread, or the tread of a wood stair as well as providing a non-slip surface.

Choose a dense weave with short tufts that will withstand heavy stairway traffic. Some natural fibers, such as sisal, coir, and jute, are also a good choice as they are tough, resilient, and keep their good looks even when subject to heavy wear. However, some natural fibers, such as sea grass, are naturally slippery and not suitable for stairs.

Stairways and landings are very often fitted with the same floor covering, and this is sometimes even carried through into the bedrooms which visually opens up the space for a cohesive finish.

▶ **Soft touches**
Wooden floorboards throughout the house are cushioned on the landings by classic Persian rugs which both delineate the landing space and give a softness to the whole interior.

▶▶ **Creative contrast**
Here, the traffic area of the landing is finished in soft yellow stone, contrasting it with the dark stained wooden floor elsewhere. This not only makes for a striking color scheme, it also divides the space, adding to the overall intimacy.

ARCHWAYS, CORBELS & STAIR BRACKETS

Although people are always passing through connecting spaces, rather than resting in and appreciating them, these are where some of the richest architectural embellishments can be seen. When you enter the front door, you may see an elaborate plaster-decorated arch set partway down the hall, featuring reed-and-tie pilasters and visually framing the stairway. In more modest houses, this archway is likely to be purely symbolic and limited to the ceiling area where elaborate corbels hold up plaster-decorated ceiling panels. Look up and you'll often see some of the richest ceiling moldings featuring plaster blocks with flower-like motifs similar to miniature ceiling medallions. Walk down by the side of the stairs and you could see exquisitely carved strings—carved stair brackets that support the risers.

▶ Attention to detail
Exquisite plaster moldings at the top of the columns, elegant key design detailing on the cornice, and pretty stair brackets testify to the attention to detail traditionally given to period halls.

◀ ▼ Enhance what you have
Plaster or wooden details need not be limited to walls. Here they appear on the edge of the staircase in a style particularly redolent of the early twentieth century.

▼ Pillar power
Elaborate plaster pillars and archways are often positioned partway down the hallway, giving visual interest as you look toward the front door. These exquisite fluted pilasters with acanthus-decorated capitols are especially fine.

HANDRAILS

Tracing a smooth run from the top of the house to the ground floor, handrails make a strong visual statement while introducing an irresistibly tactile element to the house. An elegant winding stairway is the hallmark of the grandest of period homes, its serpentine handrail curving down through the center of the house. But today, more houses have dog-leg, or "split-landing," staircases with newel posts on each landing so the handrail is made in straight runs These may not be as beguiling as winding handrails, but they are less expensive and require less exact engineering than their winding counterparts. Many wooden handrails are stripped and polished so they stand out against white balusters, making an excellent hallway focus. Metal handrails offer more design scope as they can be cast or wrought into fine shapes—perfect for modern spiral or elliptical stairways.

▲ Fine metal

Wrought iron can be worked into fine shapes to create a sophisticated handrail like this, which delicately weaves its way down from the top to the bottom of the house.

▲ Smooth sweep

The handrails of this sweeping Federal stairway have different profiles as they sweep downward. Overall, they give a dancing impression which seems to move as the perspective changes, depending on where you are on the landing or stairway.

◄ Modern movement

The chunky profile of the handrail of this metal spiral stair makes a positive statement in a Modern home.

BALUSTRADES

Balusters and newel posts support the handrail, together making up the balustrade. The supports are usually, but certainly not always, vertical and indeed, some of the most elegant balusters run laterally, bringing an almost nautical appeal to the stairway. Running down through the whole of the house, balustrades have a huge impact on the architecture on all floors of the home. The balusters can be unassuming and square in profile, intricately turned, or fashioned with fretwork into endless designs.

Metal offers even more choices as the material can be cast into dramatic shapes or wrought into pretty filigree designs. It is generally better to restore original balustrades rather than to cover them up or change them, as this can dramatically affect the architecture of the whole house. Damaged sections of both wooden and metal balustrades can be matched and replaced by joiners and metal workers respectively, quickly restoring the house to its original glory.

▶▶ Straight talking
These fine, straight balusters set in pairs down the stairs bring a light and airy feel to the hallway. Here, the look is cleanly Modern, but straight, square-profile balusters were also typical in Federal houses.

▶ Star turn
Balusters of fretwork like this always add individuality to the home. Although they look solid, the pretty star and teardrop motifs are delightful feminine details.

BEDROOMS

pretty

personal

ceilings

fireplaces

storage

pattern

feminine

soft

carpet

private

intimate

MASTER STYLE

Upstairs, it is in the master bedroom that architectural embellishments are designed to look beautiful and also be arresting. In period houses, this is where the crown moldings, picture rails, and chair rails are planned to look charming; the windows generous; and the fireplaces elaborate.

Before central heating became the norm in the twentieth century, fireplaces were a necessity in all the bedrooms, so they became the focus of the room. In grand master bedrooms, they were often made of elaborately carved marble featuring delicate garlands, swags, and fine pilasters, depending on the period, while tiny attic rooms were endowed with much smaller fireplaces to suit the needs of the room. Their slim proportions and simple decoration gave them a charm of their own.

▼ **Cool and clear**

Designed around the proportions of a king-size bed, this bedroom has been endowed with interest by fine architectural detailing. The wall behind the bed has been beautified by neat paneling and glass panels at either side. The floor in dark-stained wood provides a much softer and more intimate feel than the cool, white tile outside on the landing.

The vaulted ceiling has been plastered and painted white to create as great a sense of space as possible.

Elaborate key-style cornicing is typical of the Federal period. This bold cornice adds to the importance of the vaulted ceiling.

Louvered shutters on the windows can be adjusted to allow light through or to block it out. Painted white, they give the room a cool, airy look, while adding texture to the interior.

A pale loop-pile carpet is fitted wall to wall for a cohesive finish, and it provides a soft surface when stepping out of bed.

◀ **Fine show**

Exquisite original architectural embellishments, like this elaborate cornice, are features worth emphasizing. This is achieved here simply by painting the walls in a contrasting azure blue to set them off.

BEDROOMS

Apart from the fireplace, the tradition in the eighteenth and nineteenth centuries was to generally save embellishments for the areas of the house that were on display. This meant that, certainly in row houses, the higher the floor, the less architecturally decorative the rooms became. However, by the mid-twentieth century, bedrooms were no longer the second-class citizens of the house. This was partly because the detail throughout the house was much plainer anyway, devoid of extraneous embellishments, such as chair and picture rails; even crown moldings were beginning to disappear. Bedrooms at last found themselves on an equal footing with the rest of the house. In contemporary homes, the styling is much simpler, and the options have opened up to include an uncluttered look with wall-to-wall closets hiding the clothes and sundries that are all part of bedroom necessity. A beautiful bed taking center stage in a well-proportioned space with simple detailing is the perfect recipe for an oasis of calm in which to relax at the end of a stressful day.

▲ Grand design
The master bedroom in period homes was often endowed with elaborate cornices like this one, which provides a striking border for the vaulted ceiling.

◀ Perfect plan

This peaceful haven has all you need for a Modern bedroom. The space remains uncluttered, thanks to plenty of storage for clothes, books, and even a television, yet fine detailing means it's far from sterile. Frameless doors offer a clear view of the patio beyond, and a fuss-free fireplace adds architectural interest.

BEDROOM WALLS

Even if sleek paint is the only finish you'd consider elsewhere in the house, the bedroom is the one room where you may feel more adventurous. This is the space where you can afford to be at your most feminine, possibly using decorative wallpaper and borders, or painting on motifs using stamps or stencils. All these are in strong American tradition, following in the footsteps of artisans in Colonial times who would travel around the land, taking commissions to add decorative detail to walls throughout the house.

As well as traditional wallpaper, there are increasing choices in new coverings. Some are designed so that strong colors or panels of color can be juxtaposed to create interesting geometric designs. Others can be individually created using favorite photographs or images, blown up and printed on wallpaper for an individual look.

▲ Period charm
Cream antique paneling adds some delightful feminine charm to this bedroom, enhancing the wall behind the bedstead.

▶ Paint it strong
Paint can be mixed to any shade, and if the walls are in good condition, it is relatively easy to change. So be bold. Paint the walls in this year's color to off-set the architectural detailing, as in this crisp but feminine bedroom.

▶▶ Pattern perfection
Wallpaper is the easiest way to bring pattern to the walls, especially if you check the effect by pinning up a single length before making the purchase. Based on an eighteenth-century French design, this toile de Jouy has a classic elegance.

FLOOR TREATMENTS

Going barefoot in the bedroom means that most of us prefer our flooring to be on the soft side. In cooler climes, wall-to-wall carpeting is frequently installed on top of original wooden floorboards for warmth, comfort, and insulation. The bedroom suffers the least wear in the house, so this is always a highly practical solution, and you can choose from many varieties of pile (see page 69). However, with central heating universally used during the twentieth century, many people felt it was a shame to continue covering up beautiful original floors, so they opted instead to strip back the carpets and use large rugs that brought softness to most of the room while setting off glowing wooden boards. In hotter zones where the floors are more likely to be cool ceramic tiles, an attractive bedside rug is all that is needed to soften the first steps of the morning.

▶ **Two-tier luxury**
The Seventies style of using luxurious deep-pile rugs, such as Greek flokati, sheepskin, or shag pile on top of wall-to-wall velvet carpet, is seeing a revival in the twenty-first century.

▼ **Cool solution**
Here, a cool ceramic floor is softened by a simple woven cotton rug at each side of the bed, bringing interest to the floor of this Spanish-style bedroom.

BEDROOM CLOSETS

Keeping clothes, shoes, accessories, spare bedding, and lotions and potions under control requires plenty of planning. You can choose the traditional way, furnishing your bedroom with beautiful antique armoires and chests of drawers, or go the Modern route of building in storage to suit your individual needs. The built-in option makes the best use of the space, and with many firms offering this as a specialty, there is no shortage of closet designs from which to choose. Select from sleek, minimal closet doors, disguised as the walls themselves, with secret hinges and invisible handles. Or if you have a period house, you may prefer to have closets designed to blend with the rest of the architecture of the room by adding trimwork at ceiling level and baseboards at floor level.

Whatever the design, it is well worth thinking carefully about how you would like the insides divided. Do you prefer mainly hanging space or stacking space? How high do you want the hanging rail? Could you fit one rail above the other to accommodate two levels of hanging shirts, jackets or trousers, for example? Or do you need some full-length hanging space? How do you plan to deal with shoes and accessories? The more ordered your plan, the better everything will fit in and the more organized you can be about putting away and finding your clothes. This, in turn, will have an impact on how neat you can keep your bedroom.

▶ Behind closed doors

Floor-to-ceiling and wall-to-wall, these closets almost look like walls themselves, yet they provide voluminous hanging and storage space.

▶▶ Vanity flair

Traditional dressing tables are still hugely useful pieces of bedroom furniture. As well as providing somewhere for a lady to attend to her toilette, the drawers and cabinets offer storage space for jewelry, makeup, and hairbrushes, so that they are all at hand when they are needed.

▲ Inside story

The organization of the insides of closets is just as important as the design of the outside. This walk-in closet has a double bank of hanging rails, providing plenty of storage for shirts and jackets. The unit next to them has been divided into cubes, perfectly sized for folded garments and individual pairs of shoes for swift selection and easy arranging.

BEDROOM SHUTTERS

Shutters in the bedroom provide ultimate privacy while ensuring the early morning sun does not get the chance to disturb your slumber. Solid or paneled shutters are traditional in the cooler regions, as they provide insulation against the cold night air. In the warmer states, louvered shutters provide the best solution as the louvers can be opened or closed to allow for cool air to circulate and to shield the room from glaring midday sun while still letting in some light. However, this distinction has blurred over the course of time and fashion. As long ago as the Early Federal period, louvered shutters were installed even in houses in the more northern states. Whichever you choose, shutters bring architectural interest to the bedroom, while imparting a sense of privacy and intimacy.

▶ **Adjustable light**
Divided, folding shutters like these provide ultimate flexibility, especially when the louvers themselves can be individually opened and closed. The shutters and louvers can be adjusted as the sun moves around, thereby eliminating the glare without plunging the room into darkness.

▲ **New interpretation**
Louvered shutters work well in Modern homes as their neat, geometric lines suit clean, simple interiors while adding architectural interest.

BEDROOM CEILINGS

Often located at the top of the house, bedroom architecture frequently includes exposed ceiling trusses, beams, rafters, and posts. It can also feature under-eave slopes, dormer windows, and roof lights, all of which make for interesting ceilings. The decision lies in whether to expose, hide, or make features of these elements. Generally, they add charm to the room, and should be seen as features rather than hindrance to the overall design. For this reason, when decorating upper rooms, make these features your starting point, ensuring that any beams are in good condition, and if they are to be exposed, deciding whether you'd like them stripped, painted, or stained. This will set the style for the rest of the room.

▲▶ Smooth groove
A board ceiling works particularly well in cottage-style attic bedrooms. It is practical, too, making an ideal solution for covering up rafters or uneven surfaces.

▶ Cottage charm
Where rafters are exposed, they can readily be turned into a feature with the application of a dark stain, creating that charming cottage style.

▲ Top treatment

Rather than trying to hide the support structure at the top of the house, you can make a feature of it, as here, where a plaster panel featuring a cupid and acanthus leaves decorates the roof support.

◀ Natural choice

The stripped beams of this Spanish-style room match the stripped wooden lintels and window frames, bringing architectural charm to the room.

BATHROOMS

clean

luxury

splash

faucets

steam

shiny

spa

marble

ceramics

glass

fresh

CLEAN SIMPLICITY

An atmosphere of billowing steam, condensation, and torrents of water demands special architectural needs. Bathroom embellishments must be water resistant and, preferably, easy to wipe down. Practicality aside, we all want our bathrooms to look almost clinically clean. Grime-harboring nooks and crevices are conducive neither to the enjoyment of a quick refreshing shower, nor to the leisurely luxury of a perfume-filled bath in our own private spa. Another important consideration is that bathroom space is often limited. In modern homes, the number of bathrooms matters more than their size. One per bedroom arranged en suite is the ideal. All this means that many Modern bathroom embellishments are sleek and have a streamlined look that makes best use of the limited space.

Bathrooms in period homes are traditionally furnished in a more decorative way that reflects the architecture in the rest of the house. The typical Victorian bathtub was made from cast iron with claw feet and served by elaborate faucets (see opposite). Plumbing was still exposed, though this could be incorporated into the design with, for example, tall brass pipes for the faucets, set into the floor rather than on the bath.

▶ **Period pretty**

Period bathrooms were often furnished with a freestanding cast-iron, claw-foot bathtub, like this one. It's a look that still has appeal today, but relies on a room at least the size of a single bedroom.

▶▶ **Bathed in nostalgia**

A claw-foot cast-iron bath takes center stage in this grand Victorian-style bathroom, giving it a furnished, rather than fitted look. Nineteenth-century houses did not always include bathrooms, and as running water became standard, a bedroom was often set aside as a washroom. Sometimes, a fireplace remains, betraying the original purpose of the room.

▲ **Freestanding flair**

Positioning the tub in the center of the room requires ample space, but the result is the ultimate in bathing luxury. Faucets set on tall, shiny chrome pipes add a sculptural element to the room.

The crown molding reflects those used in other upstairs rooms in the house, providing the bathroom with a sense of grandeur.

The elegant, tall cabinet is ideal for storing bathroom paraphernalia, ranging from towels and face cloths on upper levels, to medical and dental needs in the middle, and cleaning equipment on the lower shelves. The freestanding nature of the furniture keeps it in style with the overall look of the room.

A simple glass shelf makes an ideal wipe-clean surface in any bathroom.

Brass telephone-handle faucet sets are typically Victorian, bringing a shiny accessorized touch to the bathroom.

The claw-foot, cast-iron bath is typical of the era, and with both ends rounded, is often placed in the center of the room. Looking more like a piece of furniture than a contemporary paneled bath, it has enjoyed a revival in recent decades.

A polished marble floor is waterproof and light reflective, making it the perfect bathroom choice.

Vanity units were often a modern-day interpretation of the old washstands.

Bathroom lighting has always needed special consideration. Fixtures have to be completely sealed to be made waterproof and positioned to give ample, preferably flattering light to facilitate efficient shaving and makeup application. Modern recessed lighting has perfectly fulfilled this role, offering a choice of fixed or adjustable styles.

And as for mirrors, these have an important role in bathroom embellishment. Not only are they a necessity of one's daily toilet, but their reflective quality can transform what is often a small dark room into one that appears to be both larger and lighter.

▲ In the round
Flush surfaces keep this circular bathroom sleek. Tall bath faucets bring architectural interest.

▶ Minimal and Modern
A cantilevered vanity unit, free of embellishment, makes an ideal solution in this Modern bathroom. With an uncluttered stainless-steel basin and minimal faucets, it looks clean and sleek and makes the very best use of space. Complemented by the similarly styled mirror, these simple elements add up to an elegant, Modern bathroom.

▲ Room for the bath

The original bathroom in some older period houses was often located in an inconvenient part of the home—for example, next to the kitchen. But later, one of the bedrooms was often converted instead. Here, the result has a furnished look echoing the style of the rest of the house.

▲▶ All white

White is an excellent bathroom choice as most fixtures are available in white, and there are plenty of surfaces in splash-proof and waterproof materials, such as rubber, marble, and vinyl.

▶ Tile style

Not all bathroom surfaces have to be waterproof, but those around the wet areas do, offering plenty of scope for interesting walls. Here, they have been tiled from the floor to the top of the backsplash, and the wall above is painted.

BATHROOM FLOORS

This, the wettest room in the house, should ideally have a floor that can withstand splashes at least, floods at worst. For this reason, the most suitable floors are either stone or ceramic, sealed with waterproof grout. However, there are plenty of other choices. If you like the look of wood, you can use boards treated with yacht varnish, or have a latticework of an oily wood, such as teak, set over a gully for efficient drainage in case of flood. Bamboo is another excellent material for bathroom floors as it is naturally waterproof and looks great. There are suitable resilient floors, too, such as rubber or liquid vinyl, which is poured on-site, then allowed to set in position.

Carpet was popular toward the end of the twentieth century when special rubber-backed grades were introduced, offering an enviable luxurious and soft underfoot feel when stepping out of the bath. However, the practicality of hard and resilient floors, combined with their attractive good looks, make them the current bathroom standard.

▲ Standing stone

The soft, buttery tones of limestone make it a perennial bathroom floor favorite. This one has been laid with matching limestone edging and an integral drain in the floor: the perfect safeguard against flooding.

◄ Ceramic chic

These ceramic tiles made to look like limestone are more scratch resistant than the stone original. Here, they have been laid herringbone-style for visual interest.

◄◄ Magnificent marble

This elegant marble floor with its pale, veined tones is the ideal bathroom solution, being water resistant while teaming well with white bathroom suites.

BATHROOM FAUCETS

Modern technology has meant the design of faucets can be neater and more streamlined than their predecessors, and fashions have changed from Victorian curves to ever-sleeker models. In their most minimal form, bath faucets can simply be a single-lever pillar that controls both the temperature and flow of water, delivered through a "bath filler" in the side of the tub, rather than a spout.

The choice in bathroom faucets can be bewildering as they come in many forms, such as one-hole monoblocks, three-hole (hot, cold, and spout), even four-hole (hot, cold, shower, and spout). They can be floor mounted (baths), wall mounted, bath or basin mounted, or even worktop mounted (basins). Shower faucets offer an even more complicated menu of choices, as they need to control the thermostat and flow for fixed showerheads and handheld showers. The solution is not to buy in a hurry. Research the general style you like, make an initial trip to the bathroom showroom, and carefully consider the options available to you before returning to buy. Whatever you eventually choose, try to buy the whole "suite" of faucets for basins, bath, and shower together for a final, coordinated look.

▶ **Trouble-free fixtures**
These streamlined, modern faucets made from crisp chrome are three-hole, wall-mounted versions. With a lever for both hot and cold water, the flow and temperature of the water can be easily regulated.

▼ **Traditional styling**
Traditional-style basin faucets finished in brass have simple, hand-turn valves and a swan-neck spout with a pop-up drain, which dispenses with cumbersome plugs on chains that can easily break.

▶ **Period elegance**
Imposing Edwardian-style bath faucets are floor mounted and finished in shiny chrome to make a statement in any style of bathroom.

▲ Sublimely easy
This elegant, two-hole faucet consists of a swan-neck spout and single lever that controls the flow and temperature of the water.

◀ Stately grandeur
The brass faucets and mixer tap are entirely in keeping with their surroundings, enhancing the ornate details on the washstand.

BATHROOM WALLS

Not all bathroom walls have to be splash-proof, water-proof and damp-proof—but around the basin, bath, and shower areas, they certainly do. The rest of the walls can be simply wipe-clean paint or paper. Ceramic tiles have been the traditional solution since Roman times, and with the unlimited variety of color, finish (matte or shiny), and size (squares to 2 x 2 feet or more), there sometimes seems little reason to change. With such a wide range of choice, there is plenty of scope for design flair, too. Tiles can be laid in the regular way, diagonally, or, if they are rectangular, brick bond style. Grout can match or contrast with the tiles. You may choose coordinating border tiles, or contrasting tile borders.

In addition to ceramic, there are plenty of other choices of material. Glass mosaic tiles, for example, have been a popular bathroom wall choice since Roman times, too. Now they have been joined by much larger glass tiles, glass screens, and glass bricks. Another idea to add texture around the lower part of the room is to use beaded board paneling in wet areas, finished with a yacht varnish or a similarly robust paint.

▲ Bright idea

Glazed ceramic mosaics in peacock blue lend a rich feel to a tiny bathroom.

◄ Alternative glass

Glass is an ideal waterproof material that does not have to be restricted to windows. A glass brick wall is the perfect splashback, yet lets in plenty of light from outside, while colored glass creates a stylish modern wall between the bath and shower areas.

◄◄ Pretty paneling

Tongue-and-groove paneling painted in gloss or eggshell paint is robust enough to protect the wet areas, yet it brings a soft, furnished feel to the room.

BATHROOM SURFACES

The need for splash-proof surfaces for bathrooms is not as limiting as it may at first seem. The surfaces will be splashed but there is not the risk, as there is with the floor, of flooding, so the material will not be subject to long-term soaking. Marble and ceramic tiles have long been a bathroom surface favorite, but since the second half of the twentieth century, vanity units have often been given laminate tops of various types. In recent years, glass and even stainless steel have become popular, but they need regular wiping to keep them clear of unsightly splashes. This is a trick you could never try with polished wood, which would quickly become watermarked. However, oiled wood is splash-proof, and can be simply wiped down with a damp cloth, making it a practical and beautiful natural bathroom surface.

▲ Cool combinations
Because of its elegant pale tones, its cool touch, and the fact that it can be cut to any shape, marble has long been a favorite bathroom surface.

▶ Light fantastic
Glass has become a popular bathroom surface as it provides a wonderful light and airy feel to the whole room.

◀ Made to measure
Granite can be cut to any shape, so it is perfect for bathrooms as it can be made to accommodate any shape or size of basin and any faucet combination.

PHOTOGRAPHY CREDITS

The publisher would like to thank the following photographers for supplying the pictures in this book:

Page 1 Michel Arnaud; **2** Grey Crawford; **3** Peter Margonelli; **4** bottom Fernando Bengoechea; **4** top Jeremy Samuelson; **5 bottom** William Waldron; **5 top** Peter Margonelli; **6** Gordon Beall; **8** Gordon Beall; **9** Tim Street-Porter; **10** Jacques Dirand; **11** Joshua McHugh; **12** Simon McBride; **13** Oberto Gili; **14** Tim Beddow; **15** Tria Giovan; **16** Gordon Beall; **17 bottom** Grazia Branco; **17 top** Jonn Coolidge; **19** John M. Hall; **20 top** William Waldron; **21** Jonn Coolidge; **22** Thibault Jeanson; **24** Oberto Gili; **25** Tria Giovan; **26** Tria Giovan; **28 top** Tim Street-Porter; **29** Paul Whicheloe; **32 top** Toshi Otsuki; **33** Jan Tham; **34** Courtesy of *House Beautiful*; **36 top** Oberto Gili; **37** Oberto Gili; **38** Oberto Gili; **40 top** Tim Street-Porter; **41** Tria Giovan; **42** Tria Giovan; **44 top** Jeff Goldberg; **45** Anthony Cotsifas; **46** Richard Bryant/Arcaid; **48** Victoria Pearson; **49** William Waldron; **50** Michel Arnaud; **51** Grazia Branco; **52** Eric Roth; **54** Antoine Bootz; **56** Peter Margonelli; **58** Antoine Bootz; **60** Jerome Darblay; **62** Tria Giovan; **64** J. Savage Gibson; **66** Jeff McNamara; **68** Gordon Beall; **70** Thibault Jeanson; **72** Robert Starkoff; **73** Pauld Whicheloe; **74** Oberto Gili; **75** Maurice Rougemont; **76** Tim Street-Porter; **77 bottom** René Stoeltie; **77 top** Peter Margonelli; **78** Fernando Bengoechea; **80 bottom** Timothy Hursley; **80 top** Peter Aaron/Esto; **81** Gordon Beall; **82** Gordon Beall; **83 bottom** Michael Moran; **83 top** Scott Frances; **84 left** Christophe Dugied; **84 right** Jonn Coolidge; **85** Tim Beddow; **86** bottom Grey Crawford; **86 top** William Waldron; **87 bottom** Bruce Buck; **87 top** Jacques Dirand; **88 left** Grey Crawford; **88 right** Gordon Beall; **89** Carlos Domenech; **90** Andreas von Einsiedel; **91** Jonn Coolidge; **92** Eric Biasecki; **93 bottom** Richard Felber; **93 top** Grazia Branco; **94** Timothy Hursley; **95** Richard Bryant/Arcaid; **96 bottom** Grey Crawford; **96 top** Scott Frances; **97** John M. Hall; **98 bottom left** Caroline Arber; **98 bottom right** Jonn Coolidge; **98 top right** Tom McWilliam; **99** Tria Giovan; **100 left** Tom Crane; **100 right** Eric Boman; **101 bottom** Laura Moss; **101 top** Courtesy of *House Beautiful* **102 bottom** Tria Giovan; **102 top** Scott Frances; **103 bottom** Jonn Coolidge; **103 top** Tom Crane; **104 left** John M. Hall; **104 right** Tom McWilliam; **105 bottom** Keith Scott Morton; **105 top** Timothy Hursley; **106** Antoine Bootz; **107** Jeremy Samuelson; **108 left** Eric Biasecki; **108 righ**t Scott Frances; **109 bottom** Nedjeljko Matura; **109 top** Scott Frances; **110 left** Tria Giovan; **110 right** Fernando Bengoechea; **111** Caroline Arber; **112** Oberto Gili; **113 bottom** Steven Randazzo; **113 top** Jonn Coolidge; **114** Simon Upton; **115** Michel Arnaud; **116** Alex Hemer; **117** Tria Giovan; **118 left** Tim Street-Porter; **118 right** Gordon Beall; **119** Christophe Dugied; **120** Gordon Beall; **121** Grey Crawford; **122 left** Jeff McNamara; **122 right** Jeff McNamara; **123** Michel Arnaud; **124 left** Scott Frances; **124 right** Jonn Coolidge; **125** Fernando Bengoechea; **126** Oberto Gili; **127** William Waldron; **128** Tria Giovan; **129 bottom** William Waldron; **129 top** Pierre Chanteau; **130** Scott Frances; **131** Eric Boman; **132** Eric Boman; **133** Peter Margonelli; **134 bottom** Jonn Coolidge; **134 top** Thibault Jeanson; **135** Dana Gallagher; **136** John Ellis; **137** Tim Street-Porter; **138 bottom** Michael Moran; **138 top** Oberto Gili; **139** Jonn Coolidge; **140** Carlos domenech; **141** Jacques Dirand; **142 bottom** William Waldron; **142 top** Oberto Gili; **143 bottom** Tria Giovan; **143 top** Scott Frances; **144** Francois Dischinger; **145 bottom** Courtesy of *House Beautiful*; **145 top** Richard Bryant/Arcaid; **146 bottom** Oberto Gili; **146 top** Courtesy of *House Beautiful*; **147** Tim Street-Porter; **148 left** Courtesy of *House Beautiful*; **148 right** Scott Frances; **149 bottom** Gordon Beall; **149 top left** Thibault Jeanson; **149 top right** Oberto Gili; **150 left** Jonn Coolidge; **150 right** Tim Street-Porter; **151** Image Studios; **152 left** Courtesy of *House Beautiful*; **152 righ**t Peter Margonelli; **153 bottom** Luca Trovato; **153 top left** Image Studios; **153 top right** Peter Margonelli; **154 left** William Waldron; **154 right** Daniel Aubrey; **155** Jonn Coolidge; **156 left** William Waldron; **156 right** Jonn Coolidge; **157** Fernando Bengoechea.

INDEX